THE
SEARCH
FOR
SIGNIFICANCE

DEVOTIONAL
JOURNAL

THE
SEARCH
FOR
SIGNIFICANCE

DEVOTIONAL
JOURNAL

Based on *The Search for Significance*

ROBERT S. McGEE

W PUBLISHING GROUP™

www.wpublishinggroup.com

A Division of Thomas Nelson, Inc.
www.ThomasNelson.com

Published by W Publishing Group, a Division of Thomas Nelson, Inc., P.O. Box 141000, Nashville, Tennessee 37214.

Produced with the assistance of The Livingstone Corporation (www.LivingstoneCorporation.com). Project staff includes Dave Veerman, Betsy Schmitt, and Carol Ochs. Devotional questions written by Carol Smith.

Library of Congress Cataloging-in Publication Data

McGee, Robert S.
    The search for significance devotional journal / by Robert S. McGee.
      p. cm.
    ISBN 0-8499-4427-9
    1. Self-esteem—Religious aspects—Christianity. 2. Christian life. 3. Devotional calendars. I. Title.
    BV4647.S43M394 2003
    248.4--dc21

2003005823

Printed in the United States of America

05 06 07 RRD 9 8 7 6 5 4 3

INTRODUCTION

If making positive changes in our lives were as easy as simply reading something, recognizing the truth in what we've read, and then seeing our lives instantly change at the recognition of that truth, life would be much more enjoyable. However, it's not that easy, as we all know. God warns us that we must lay off the "old man" and put on the "new man." We must tear down strongholds in order to bring our thoughts into obedience to Christ (which is going to be the occasion when we see our lives really change).

This takes place over time. Over the next few weeks, even years, God is going to allow you to encounter opportunities to rely on the truths presented in *The Search for Significance*. Your response to these situations will not change God's love and acceptance of you or your eternal union with Him. However, the Father is serious about preparing you, His child, for eternity. He wants to weed out the hurtful, painful strongholds that are currently robbing you of the life Christ has provided. And that's where this devotional journal comes in. It is designed to help you put yourself in a place where God can begin to work on you and break down those strongholds.

To get the most out of this devotional journal, you will want to first make sure you've read *The Search for Significance*, for in that book you'll discover the foundational principles for this sixty-day guided journal. If it's been awhile since you've read *The Search for Significance*, you may even want to go back and reread it before you dive into this journal.

Don't get caught up in being legalistic about your journaling; that is, don't beat yourself up if you miss a day or two every so often. But at the same time, realize that completing this journal will be in your best self-interest, for by the time you've finished it, you will not only comprehend more clearly the breadth of Christ's love for you, but you'll also experience what it means to walk in the freedom of that love. The more you are able to put on the "new man," the easier it will be to win out over the "old man."

Today, more than ever, Christians need to know who they are and the victory they have in Christ. My hope and prayer is that this devotional journal will take you one step closer toward gaining that knowledge and experiencing that victory.

—ROBERT MCGEE

WHO HAS THE ANSWER I'M LOOKING FOR?

And He said, "Therefore I have said to you that no one can come to
Me unless it has been granted to him by My Father."

From that time many of His disciples went back and walked
with Him no more. Then Jesus said to the twelve, "Do you also
want to go away?"

But Simon Peter answered Him, "Lord, to whom shall we go?
You have the words of eternal life. Also we have come to believe and
know that You are the Christ, the Son of the living God."

—JOHN 6:65–69

KNOWING THE RIGHT QUESTION

> **What are the various reasons people search for their worth
> anywhere else but in God?**

Whether labeled *self-esteem* or *self-worth*, the feeling of significance
is crucial to man's emotional, spiritual, and social stability and is the
driving element within the human spirit. Understanding this single
need opens the door to understanding our actions and attitudes.

What a waste to attempt to change behavior without truly understanding the driving needs that cause such behavior! Yet millions of people spend a lifetime searching for love, acceptance, and success without understanding the need that compels them. We must understand that this hunger for self-worth is God-given and can only be satisfied by Him. Our value is not dependent on our ability to earn the fickle acceptance of people, but rather, its true source is the love and acceptance of God. He created us. He alone knows how to fulfill all of our needs.

Think over the past twenty-four hours. When did you feel most valuable? Describe those situations.

What would be different in your life if you walked around with that valuable feeling all the time? What would this world be like if people everywhere felt valued?

In John 6:65–69 Simon Peter came to the place each of us hopefully comes to—God is the only one who has the answers. It just takes us awhile sometimes to start asking the right questions. How does God answer the question of what makes you valuable?

Today, right now, in this moment, what do you *feel* you're worth? On what are you basing your answer?

TALK TO GOD

Heavenly Father, it takes time for me to sort through all the things I think I need in order to get down to my most basic needs. Sometimes the small things in life cause me to scurry past the important stuff. I give myself to You. Here I am for You to help me see what my most basic needs are so that I will know that You are the source for all I need. Help me this day not to give in to the temptation to find those answers anywhere else. Amen.

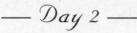

— Day 2 —

IS IT REALLY DARKEST BEFORE THE DAWN?

I am continually with You; You hold me by my right hand. You will guide me with Your counsel, and afterward receive me to glory.

Whom have I in heaven but You? And there is none upon earth that I desire besides You. My flesh and my heart fail; but God is the strength of my heart and my portion forever.

—Psalm 73:23–26

EXPOSING THE WOUNDS

If it were easy to be honest with yourself, words like *denial* wouldn't be used so often. That's why we need God's help sometimes to get gut-level honest before Him. Write a prayer giving God access to your most innermost thoughts and feelings. Ask Him to help you be totally honest in this process of discovering your own worth.

When the light of love and honesty shines on thoughts of hopelessness, it is often very painful. We begin to admit that we really do feel negatively about ourselves—and have for a long time. But God's love, expressed through His people and woven into our lives by His Spirit and His Word, can, over a period of time, bring healing even to our deepest wounds and instill within us an appropriate sense of self-worth.

Ask the Lord to give you the courage to be honest. Give Him permission to shine His Spirit's light on your thoughts, feelings, and actions. You may be surprised by additional pain as you realize the extent of your wounds, but our experience of healing can only be as deep as our awareness of the need for it. This takes the power of God's light. Ask Him to turn on the light.

When the light does come on in our lives, we will discover that we have tried to meet certain needs in the wrong way. It isn't that the needs are not real, it is just that we have tried to meet these needs in inappropriate ways.

Our self-worth is at our very core. It's a scary journey. We often try other avenues first to feel good about ourselves: attempts at perfection, one-upmanship, people-pleasing, even invisibility. What are some of the tactics that you've tried to make you feel good about yourself? What has been the result?

According to Psalm 73, we can trust God even more than we can trust ourselves. What difference would it make in your life to trust God's opinion of you over your own?

All of us have wounds. It's part of being human. Think about what made you angry over the last twenty-four hours. Some of our anger is connected to old wounds, which is why it's painful to explore. What is the last thing you can remember that made you angry?

How is what made you angry related to old wounds you still may carry?

Because you've invited God into this process with you, He is working in your life. In these next few days, let God use the situations or people that spark emotion in you to reveal old wounds that He would like to heal. What do you look forward to or dread in this journey of self-discovery and God-discovery?

TALK TO GOD

Holy God, when life gets difficult it's easy to believe that I'm just doing it wrong. It's easy to think, when things are painful, that I need to make it better right away by getting busy or taking something for the pain or simply running away. Father, help me to sit with You as we sift through these troubled places in my life. When You bring to light something difficult, help me to trust You enough to stay by Your side and let You clean and heal my wounds. Thank You for Your healing. Amen.

WHERE DO YOU THINK YOU'RE GOING?

Examine me, O LORD, and prove me; try my mind and my heart. For Your lovingkindness is before my eyes, and I have walked in Your truth.

—PSALM 26:2–3

DEFINING THE JOURNEY

What do you hope will be accomplished by God's rummaging through your soul and helping you identify false beliefs?

From where do our destructive emotions come? Answer: Destructive thoughts. What triggers destructive thoughts? Answer: False beliefs. And how are the false beliefs energized? Answer: Our life situations.

Can we control our life situations to the degree that we can keep our false beliefs from being triggered? We try sometimes, but obviously that cannot be done. Therefore, we have a great need to destroy the false beliefs and replace them with the truth that God has disclosed to us.

We call this process The Trip In.

If our emotions come from our thoughts, and our thoughts spring from our beliefs, what is the significance of identifying your beliefs? What are the benefits?

Think over the past twenty-four hours. What strong emotions did you feel? What triggered them?

Which of the emotions you felt might be considered destructive? Why?

Think back over the past week. Who were the people and what were the circumstances that brought out negative, destructive emotions in you? What do those feelings reveal about your own thoughts and beliefs?

TALK TO GOD

Holy God, I am Yours, and I matter to You. You made me. It is within our relationship that I can find my most basic meaning in life. Teach me to base my life on that relationship. Help me to see clearly my false beliefs about my worth. Help me build a life based on Your truth. Amen.

WHAT'S YOUR NET WORTH?

"And do not fear those who kill the body but cannot kill the soul. But rather fear Him who is able to destroy both soul and body in hell. Are not two sparrows sold for a copper coin? And not one of them falls to the ground apart from your Father's will. But the very hairs of your head are all numbered. Do not fear therefore; you are of more value than many sparrows."

—MATTHEW 10:28–31

SETTING THE STANDARD

> Think over the past two or three days. Close your eyes and let the memories rise to the surface. Who are the people you've tried to please or keep happy in some way? Were you successful?

Our desire for acceptance pressures us to perform to gain praise from others. We strive for success, driving our minds and bodies harder and further, hoping that because of our sweat and sacrifice others will appreciate us more.

But the man or woman who lives only for the love and attention of others is never satisfied—at least, not for long. Despite our efforts, we will never find lasting, fulfilling peace if we must continually prove ourselves to others. Our desire to be loved and accepted is a symptom of a deeper need—the need that frequently governs our behavior and is the primary source of our emotional pain. Often unrecognized, this is our need for self-worth.

Think about the relationship between a person's desire to be loved and accepted and that person's deeper need for self-worth. As you review your last few days, what symptoms can you see in yourself that reveal your need for self-worth?

As you think about emotionally painful interactions, or even whole seasons in your life, how did those difficulties relate to your own struggle for self-worth?

Sometimes we try to gain the approval of other people to feel better about ourselves. Why might this be easier than focusing on God's approval? When has this been true for you?

Based on Matthew 10:28–31, what is your worth in God's eyes?

TALK TO GOD

Father, I will walk among people today and their opinions will matter to me. Help me to keep that in perspective. Remind me that Your opinion is what matters most. Keep Your face as real to me as the face of each person I meet. The truth is that I am of worth because You claim me to be of worth. Help me to walk in that truth today. Amen.

WHAT DOES FAILURE REALLY TEACH YOU?

[Abraham] did not waver at the promise of God through unbelief, but was strengthened in faith, giving glory to God, and being fully convinced that what He had promised He was also able to perform. And therefore "it was accounted to him for righteousness."

Now it was not written for his sake alone that it was imputed to him, but also for us. It shall be imputed to us who believe in Him who raised up Jesus our Lord from the dead, who was delivered up because of our offenses, and was raised because of our justification.

Therefore, having been justified by faith, we have peace with God through our Lord Jesus Christ, through whom also we have access by faith into this grace in which we stand, and rejoice in hope of the glory of God.

—ROMANS 4:20–5:2

FINDING GOD'S STANDARDS

Recently, when have you felt like a failure? What caused you to feel that way?

Justification means more than forgiveness of sins. In the same act of love through which God forgave our sins, He also provided for our righteousness, the worthiness to stand in God's presence. By imputing righteousness to us, God attributes Christ's worth to us. The moment we accept Christ, God declares that we are no longer condemned sinners. Instead, we are forgiven, we receive Christ's righteousness, and we are creatures who are fully pleasing to Him.

God desires for those of us who have been redeemed to experience the realities of His redemption. We are forgiven and righteous because of Christ's sacrifice; therefore, we are pleasing to God in spite of our failures. This reality can replace our fear of failure with peace, hope, and joy. Failure need not be a millstone around our necks. Neither success nor failure is the proper basis of our self-worth. Christ alone is the source of our forgiveness, freedom, joy, and purpose.

What's the difference between basing your worth on your experiences and basing your worth on what God says about you? What difference does it make in how you live?

If you had lived the last few days more in the truth of Romans 4:20–5:2 than you actually did (at peace with God, in grace through faith, rejoicing in His hope), what would have changed?

God's love for us doesn't adjust according to our current state of success or failure. Yet often our views of ourselves change according to our circumstances. How has your view of yourself been affected by events in the past forty-eight hours?

TALK TO GOD

Father God, You are far greater than any success or failure that I will ever experience. The truth is that Your approval is far more important than the opinions of those who stand on the sidelines of my life, for or against me. I want to honor You by walking in that truth. Help me to focus on Your peace, Your grace, and Your hope in my life—no matter what else may happen. Amen.

— Day 6 —

WHO DO YOU LISTEN TO?

*I have declared my ways, and You answered me; teach me Your
statutes. Make me understand the way of Your precepts; so shall I
meditate on Your wonderful works. My soul melts from heaviness;
strengthen me according to Your word. Remove from me the way of
lying, and grant me Your law graciously. I have chosen the way
of truth; Your judgments I have laid before me. I cling to Your
testimonies; O LORD, do not put me to shame! I will run the course
of Your commandments, for You shall enlarge my heart.*

—PSALM 119:26–32

DISTINGUISHING DOING FROM BEING

**Whose opinion of you do you value most? List some of those people.
Alongside each one, list an opinion that he or she holds of you.**

Isn't it amazing that we turn to others who have a perspective as
limited and darkened as our own to discover our worth! Rather than
relying on God's steady, uplifting reassurance of who we are, we
depend on others who base our worth on our ability to meet their
standards. Because our performance and ability to please others so
dominates our search for significance, we have difficulty recognizing
the distinction between our real identity and the way we behave, a

realization crucial to understanding our true worth. Our true value is not based on our behavior or the approval of others but on what God's Word says is true of us.

If we base our worth solidly on the truths of God's Word, then our behavior will often reflect His love, grace, and power. But if we base our worth on our abilities or the fickle approval of others, then our behavior will reflect the insecurity, fear, and anger that come from such instability.

As you see it right now, what does God think of you—what's His opinion?

Consider your recent interactions with people, in particular those that caused you to feel insecure, afraid, or angry. Did your reactions (in those exchanges) indicate that you were secure in your value in God's eyes? If not, what did your reactions reveal?

Our society tends to define a person by his or her vocation. When we meet someone new, we don't ask, "Who are you really?" (That might be scary!) Instead, we harmlessly ask, "What do you do?" In conversations, what do you usually say to describe yourself that makes you feel best about yourself— that makes you feel like you matter?

Why is it difficult to give up false beliefs about ourselves?
What will it take for you to submit to God's opinion of you
and give up those false beliefs?

TALK TO GOD

Lord, I confess that in many ways I have believed my own heart and
the approval of my friends and family to be more trustworthy than Your
Word. That is the human condition. Forgive me for not trusting Your
love and strength. Forgive me for submitting to the approval of other
people when I already have Your fatherly approval. Help me today to
live according to Your unconditional approval of me and not by the
approval of others. Amen.

WHO BALANCES YOUR BOOKS?

*For it pleased the Father that in [Jesus] all the fullness should dwell,
and by Him to reconcile all things to Himself, by Him, whether
things on earth or things in heaven, having made peace through the
blood of His cross.*

*And you, who once were alienated and enemies in your mind by
wicked works, yet now He has reconciled in the body of His flesh
through death, to present you holy, and blameless, and above
reproach in His sight—if indeed you continue in the faith, grounded
and steadfast, and are not moved away from the hope of the gospel
which you heard, which was preached to every creature under
heaven, of which I, Paul, became a minister.*

—COLOSSIANS 1:19–23

UNDERSTANDING GOD'S ACCEPTANCE

**Think about when you have felt rejected by coworkers,
friends, or even family. How did you feel? How do you tend to
react to rejection mentally? Emotionally? Physically?**

God's solution to the fear of rejection is based on Christ's sacrificial payment for our sins. Through this payment, we find forgiveness, reconciliation, and total acceptance through Christ. Reconciliation means that those who were enemies have become friends.

God took our sins and canceled them by nailing them to Christ's cross. In this way, God also took away Satan's power to condemn us for sin. So you see, nothing you will ever do can nullify your reconciliation and make you unacceptable to God. Our unconditional acceptance in Christ is profound, life-changing truth.

God has taken away Satan's power to condemn us for sin. Think about your sins and missteps over the last several days, and the times that you fell short in meeting God's standard. When did you give in to condemnation? Why?

According to Colossians 1:19–23, God has reconciled you through Jesus "to present you holy, and blameless, and above reproach in His sight." What does this truth mean to you?

On a typical day—let's take yesterday—in what kinds of circumstances do you tend to forget that you are completely forgiven? What do you think would help you remember your true status before God?

Christ's sacrifice is all about giving you access to God. God is all about having a relationship with those He created. God chose you into being. Think about that for a moment. What meaning does that bring to your existence?

TALK TO GOD

Father, You paid the price for my freedom and total acceptance as Your child. You paid off my debts. What a gift! But life has a way of conspiring against my acceptance of that gift. Help me to live in the truth. Give me the strength of spirit and the trust to live today as a grateful child of God. Help me to live so that my family, friends, and coworkers see evidence of this truth in me. Amen.

WHO'S TO BLAME?

For I delight in the law of God according to the inward man. But I see another law in my members, warring against the law of my mind, and bringing me into captivity to the law of sin which is in my members. O wretched man that I am! Who will deliver me from this body of death? I thank God—through Jesus Christ our Lord!

So then, with the mind I myself serve the law of God, but with the flesh the law of sin.

There is therefore now no condemnation to those who are in Christ Jesus, who do not walk according to the flesh, but according to the Spirit. For the law of the Spirit of life in Christ Jesus has made me free from the law of sin and death. For what the law could not do in that it was weak through the flesh, God did by sending His own Son in the likeness of sinful flesh, on account of sin: He condemned sin in the flesh, that the righteous requirement of the law might be fulfilled in us who do not walk according to the flesh but according to the Spirit.

—ROMANS 7:22–8:4

ACCEPTING GOD'S EVALUATION

Think over the events of the past twenty-four hours. As you run through the list, which events make you flinch a little, maybe feel some sense of regret or failure?

One of Satan's most effective lies is *Those who fail are unworthy of love and deserve to be blamed and condemned.* Each of us has probably failed badly at some point in our lives. Perhaps some particular sin or weakness has caused us to feel condemned and unworthy of love. Without the hope and healing that God can provide, our evaluation of ourselves will eventually lead to despair.

Can we overcome Satan's deceptions and reject this basis of our self-worth? Can we trust God's complete acceptance of us as His sons and daughters and allow Him to free us from our dependency on success and the approval of others? Rejecting Satan's lie and accepting God's evaluation of us leads to a renewed hope, joy, and purpose in life.

If Satan's lie is that people who fail are unworthy of love and deserve blame, how would you describe God's reality for people who fail?

Think of the last time you failed at doing something. What was your response? What blame did you give yourself? Someone else?

In Romans 7:22–8:4 Paul describes a struggle that is familiar to most of us. How do you relate to Paul's struggle and failure to do the right thing?

Think of an area of your life that you've tried to change but have been unable to so far. Imagine that God is standing in the midst of your battle with a sign that says:

WIN OR LOSE,
YOU'LL GET HOME SAFE AND SOUND.
JUST KEEP UP THE GOOD FIGHT!

What difference would that make in your battle?

TALK TO GOD

Heavenly Father, I want to accept Your evaluation of me and walk in Your love and acceptance. Still, I struggle with the condemnation that comes with the mistakes I make. Other standards call out to me, if not louder then at least nearer sometimes than Your standard of acceptance—Christ's payment for my shortfall. Teach me to pay attention to You. You really are the voice that matters most to me. Amen.

WHO'S GOING TO CLEAN UP THIS MESS?

*But now the righteousness of God apart from the law is revealed,
being witnessed by the Law and the Prophets, even the righteousness
of God, through faith in Jesus Christ, to all and on all who believe.
For there is no difference; for all have sinned and fall short of the
glory of God, being justified freely by His grace through the
redemption that is in Christ Jesus, whom God set forth as a
propitiation by His blood, through faith, to demonstrate His
righteousness, because in His forbearance God had passed over the
sins that were previously committed, to demonstrate at the present
time His righteousness, that He might be just and the justifier of the
one who has faith in Jesus.*

—ROMANS 3:21–26

GOD'S WAY OF DEALING WITH SIN

Think about someone taking the punishment for something
you did. Think about someone paying off your debt. What
feelings does that trigger in you?

Propitiation means that the wrath of someone who has been unjustly wronged has been satisfied. It is an act that soothes hostility and satisfies the need for vengeance. Providing His only begotten Son as the propitiation for our sin was the greatest possible demonstration of God's love for man. To understand God's wondrous provision of propitiation, it is helpful to remember that God cannot overlook sin, nor can He compromise by accepting sinful behavior. For God to condone even one sin would defile His holiness like smearing a white satin wedding gown with black tar. Because He is holy, God's aversion to sin is manifested in righteous anger. However, God is not only righteously indignant about sin, He is also infinitely loving.

Because He paid the penalty for our sins, and His wrath was avenged, God no longer looks upon us through the eyes of judgment. Instead, He now lavishes His love upon us. The Scriptures teach that absolutely nothing can separate us from God's love (Rom. 8:38–39). He has adopted us into a tender, intimate, and powerful relationship with Him.

How would you like your relationship with God to be different right now?

Think about the past twenty-four hours. Think about the specific situations you faced and the emotions you felt (or tried *not* to feel). How well did you live the truth that you have a "tender, intimate, and powerful" relationship with the God of the universe?

Romans 3:21–26 says that God "passed over the sins that were previously committed." How well do you let go of past mistakes?

What specific situations do you need God's help to face without feeling condemnation or shame?

TALK TO GOD

How precious, Father God, that You would make a way to open up a relationship with me. Thanks for searching me out. Thanks for forgiving my sin. Thanks for drawing me to You even when I'm finding my sense of worth in so many other things. Help me sense Your presence. Help me honor You by receiving Your forgiveness and redemption as the costly gift to You and free gift to me that it is. Amen.

IS THERE HOPE FOR ME?

For I know that in me (that is, in my flesh) nothing good dwells; for to will is present with me, but how to perform what is good I do not find. For the good that I will to do, I do not do; but the evil I will not to do, that I practice. Now if I do what I will not to do, it is no longer I who do it, but sin that dwells in me.

I find then a law, that evil is present with me, the one who wills to do good. For I delight in the law of God according to the inward man. But I see another law in my members, warring against the law of my mind, and bringing me into captivity to the law of sin which is in my members.

—ROMANS 7:18–23

MAKING A CHANGE

What attitudes, behaviors, or habits do you feel are ingrained in you?

When we base our self-worth on past failures, dissatisfaction with personal appearance, or bad habits, we often develop the false belief *I am what I am. I cannot change. I am hopeless.* This lie binds people to the hopeless pessimism associated with poor self-esteem.

"I just can't help myself," some people say. "That's the way I've always been, and that's the way I'll always be. You can't teach an old dog new tricks." We assume that others should have low expectations of us too. "You know I can't do any better than this. What do you expect?" If we excuse our failures with an attitude of hopelessness, too often our personality can become glued to the failures. Our self-image becomes no more than a reflection of our past.

Make an honest assessment of your chances to change any of the above attitudes, behaviors, or habits. On what do you base your answer?

How would you respond to those who say, "That's just the way I am. I can't change," if you believe that they really can change. If you tried to convince them of that, what arguments would you use?

In Romans 7:18–23, Paul describes not doing the good he wants to do and doing the evil he doesn't want to do. Describe the areas of your life where you feel "stuck"—the areas that feel the hardest to change. Think about life patterns—the kinds of situations that you repeatedly find yourself involved in.

Look ahead to the next day or so. Refer to your calendar or schedule if it helps. Jot down any upcoming conversations, meetings, people, or tasks that make you feel a sense of dread, fear, or even numbness because of past experiences.

If it's true that you are more than just a catalog of your past mistakes and struggles (and it is), how does knowing the "law of God" help you face those situations?

TALK TO GOD

Father God, I give my perspective to You. Change me however You will. Align my thoughts with Yours. Help me believe in Your strength to make me new. Help me submit to Your process of doing that. Give me a sense of hope based on that faith in Your ability to change me from the inside out. I want You to be pleased with me. And I want that to be enough. Amen.

HOW CAN OLD, BROKEN THINGS BECOME NEW?

Then Jesus entered and passed through Jericho. Now behold, there was a man named Zacchaeus who was a chief tax collector, and he was rich. And he sought to see who Jesus was, but could not because of the crowd, for he was of short stature. So he ran ahead and climbed up into a sycamore tree to see Him, for He was going to pass that way. And when Jesus came to the place, He looked up and saw him, and said to him, "Zacchaeus, make haste and come down, for today I must stay at your house." So he made haste and came down, and received Him joyfully. But when they saw it, they all complained, saying, "He has gone to be a guest with a man who is a sinner."

Then Zacchaeus stood and said to the Lord, "Look, Lord, I give half of my goods to the poor; and if I have taken anything from anyone by false accusation, I restore fourfold."

And Jesus said to him, "Today salvation has come to this house, because he also is a son of Abraham; for the Son of Man has come to seek and to save that which was lost."

—Luke 19:1–10

CHANGING INSIDE-OUT

Think about a time or a situation in which you were making progress in some area of your life. It could have been personal growth, a new skill, or even a relationship that was in a really good place. What does it feel like to make a change for the better?

Can God, who spoke the universe into being, make a difference in your life?

By now I hope you understand that nothing can come between what you do and God's love for you as one of His children. To overcome shame you must accept how completely God desires to make changes in your life that will free you from your past.

Perhaps we wish that during regeneration God had turned us purple or perhaps given us yellow spots. At least then we would see a difference in ourselves. However, God has gone to the trouble of communicating that He has made us brand-new inside. And now it's up to us to take Him at His Word.

Perhaps no passage in the Bible better illustrates God's regeneration than the story of Zacchaeus, a tax collector. Zacchaeus experienced the unconditional love and acceptance of Christ. As a result, he became a different person. Through Christ, Zacchaeus developed a new self-concept, new values, new goals, and new behavior.

Identify some areas of your life in which you can see that following God has changed you.

Now name some areas in which you really wish you had experienced more of a change.

Luke 19:1–10 tells us the specifics of what Zacchaeus changed in his life. He gave back money. He corrected wrongs. All after an encounter with the Savior. Think back over the last twenty-four hours. What would you like to have done differently? How can you be like Zacchaeus and do the right thing in the next twenty-four hours?

Knowing that God is on your side, and that together with Him, you are a worthwhile person with the power to change your life for the better, how can you face the day ahead differently?

TALK TO GOD

Lord, I want to be as brave as Zacchaeus. I want to look at my life in the light of Yours and make whatever changes that prompts me to make. Help me to see those changes. Help me to do whatever it takes to make them. It's easier sometimes not to look at all. You know the human heart. But to live Your abundant life I need to connect with You and the truth of whom You made me to be. Please give me the courage to do that. Amen.

— Day 12 —

WHAT DO FEELINGS HAVE TO DO WITH IT?

My soul thirsts for God, for the living God. When shall I come and appear before God? My tears have been my food day and night, while they continually say to me, "Where is your God?"

When I remember these things, I pour out my soul within me. For I used to go with the multitude; I went with them to the house of God, with the voice of joy and praise, with a multitude that kept a pilgrim feast.

Why are you cast down, O my soul? And why are you disquieted within me? Hope in God, for I shall yet praise Him for the help of His countenance.

—PSALM 42:2–5

READING EMOTIONAL ROAD SIGNS

> **Think through the past twenty-four hours. What were the various emotions you experienced during that time?**

God has given us a supernatural deception detector, the Holy Spirit, who wants to bring us to truth. However, He has also given us a natural deception detector, our emotions. Our hurtful, negative emotions are similar to the body's mechanism of creating fever. When you have an infection, your body increases your body temperature. One of the uses of that mechanism is to alert you that you are sick. We would never take medication that would eliminate this process from occurring, as we could become deathly ill without knowing what was happening. However, many of us have a preoccupation with finding ways of avoiding all hurtful emotions through alcohol, drugs, or some form of activity that keeps us active and away from thinking about what is bothering us.

The truth about emotions is that we typically don't worry too much about the positive ones—happiness, joy, contentment. But those negative ones—sadness, anger, fear—are tough to handle. We sometimes do anything to stay away from those feelings. When you feel sad or angry or fearful, how do you typically respond (inside and outside)?

According to what you've read, what are the benefits of better understanding and expressing your emotions? How does God use your emotions as tools?

How does it affect you to have to keep your emotions hidden?

Think about your upcoming day. What situations or people do you have on your agenda that are already stirring up emotions? Identify those emotions and pray for God's help in learning from them.

TALK TO GOD

Father, it's so much easier to do than to be. In the same way, it's so much easier to do than to feel. I'm not always comfortable with my emotions. Sometimes, frankly, they just make life harder. Yet You made people with emotions that are connected to our innermost selves. Help me to understand Your plan in all that. Help me to use my emotions to understand myself better, and then to better offer myself to You. Amen.

CAN YOU JUSTIFY YOUR ACTIONS?

Therefore, having been justified by faith, we have peace with God through our Lord Jesus Christ, through whom also we have access by faith into this grace in which we stand, and rejoice in hope of the glory of God. And not only that, but we also glory in tribulations, knowing that tribulation produces perseverance; and perseverance, character; and character, hope. Now hope does not disappoint, because the love of God has been poured out in our hearts by the Holy Spirit who was given to us.

For when we were still without strength, in due time Christ died for the ungodly.

—ROMANS 5:1–6

KNOWING GOD = KNOWING YOURSELF

> **Think about three people whose opinions matter to you on a daily basis. How would you describe their expectations of you?**

The point of justification is that we can never achieve perfection on this earth; even our best efforts at self-righteousness are as filthy rags to God (Isa. 64:6). Yet He loves us so much that He appointed His Son to pay for our sins and give to us His own righteousness, His perfect status before the Father.

This doesn't mean that our actions are irrelevant and that we can sin all we want. Our sinful actions, words, and attitudes grieve the Lord, but our status as holy and beloved children remains intact. In His love, He disciplines and encourages us to live godly lives—for our good and for His honor.

If we know who we are, we will not try to become someone else in order to have value and meaning in our lives. If we don't know who we are, we *will* try to become someone whom someone else wants us to be!

What happens if you don't live up to the expectations of the people you care about? How does that affect you?

If none of the people in your life had any expectations of you, or at least if you could remove the pressure from those expectations, how would you function differently?

How do you think you can best keep in touch with God's estimation of your self-worth while you're dealing with all the expectations placed on you by other people?

Think about yesterday. What motivated you the most? Demands outside of yourself or an inner knowledge of who you are and what you should do? How do you feel about the way you lived that day?

What will be the greatest pressures ahead of you tomorrow or the next day? List those and commit those situations to God. Ask for His help to remain true to who you are within those situations.

TALK TO GOD

Holy God, I am Your child—loved, cherished, sought after, justified by Your own sacrifice. I want to live my life as a person adopted and loved by God. Life gets messy, though, and sometimes I don't do that. Forgive me for trusting other people more than You to define myself. Help me hear You even when life is very loud. Help me to listen and live according to Your truth. Amen.

WHO SAYS SO?

Whenever I am afraid, I will trust in You. In God (I will praise His word), in God I have put my trust; I will not fear. What can flesh do to me?

All day they twist my words; all their thoughts are against me for evil. They gather together, they hide, they mark my steps, when they lie in wait for my life. Shall they escape by iniquity? In anger cast down the peoples, O God!

You number my wanderings; put my tears into Your bottle; are they not in Your book? When I cry out to You, then my enemies will turn back; this I know, because God is for me. In God (I will praise His word), in the LORD (I will praise His word), in God I have put my trust; I will not be afraid. What can man do to me?

—PSALM 56:3–11

TRUSTING GOD'S VOICE

On a scale of one to ten (with one being the least and ten the greatest), how do you rate yourself as a risk taker? Describe some of the riskiest things you've done lately.

Our attempts to meet our needs for success and approval fall into two broad categories: compulsiveness and withdrawal. Some people may have a compulsive desire to be in control of every situation. They are perfectionists. If a job isn't done perfectly, if they aren't dressed just right, if they aren't considered "the best" by their peers, then they work harder until they achieve that coveted status. And woe to the poor soul who gets in their way!

The other broad category is withdrawal. Those who manifest this behavior usually try to avoid failure and disapproval by avoiding risks. They won't volunteer for the jobs that offer much risk of failure. They gravitate toward people who are comforting and kind, skirting relationships that might demand vulnerability and, consequently, the risk of rejection.

Most of us exhibit some combination of the two behaviors, willing to take risks and work hard in the areas where we feel sure of success but avoiding the people and situations that may bring rejection and failure.

How would you describe the feeling of being successful?

How would you describe the feeling of failure?

What do you have to believe about yourself and about God in order to try something that might be a risk? How much "pumping up" does it take for you?

Think back over the past twenty-four hours. What choices did you *not* make because you didn't want to fail?

The truth is, in your moments of greatest failure, you are just as cherished by God and just as valuable a person, and you're probably learning something essential. If that is true, why do we dread failure so much?

TALK TO GOD

Father, I know in order for me to.grow You will push me beyond my comfort zone. Give me the courage to follow You there. Help me care more about Your opinion than anyone else's. Help me reject the lie that I can keep myself safe enough so that my sense of "mattering" will never be challenged. Help me instead to enter into life holding on to You as my source of well-being. That, in itself, is a sacrifice of obedience I can make to You. Amen.

WHAT DOES A PRINCE INHERIT FROM THE KING?

Truly my soul silently waits for God; from Him comes my salvation. He alone is my rock and my salvation; He is my defense; I shall not be greatly moved. . . .

He only is my rock and my salvation; He is my defense; I shall not be moved. In God is my salvation and my glory; the rock of my strength, and my refuge, is in God.

—PSALM 62:1–2, 6–7

Jesus answered and said to him, "If anyone loves Me, he will keep My word; and My Father will love him, and We will come to him and make Our home with him."

—JOHN 14:23

LIVING IN HIS PRESENCE

Jesus Himself said that He would make His home in us. That means we aren't separate from God trying to appease Him. Instead, we live our lives *with* Him and *through* Him. How does knowing that relate to your value as a person?

Salvation is not simply a ticket to heaven. It is the beginning of a dynamic new relationship with God. *Justification* is the doctrine that explains the judicial facts of our forgiveness and righteousness in

Christ. *Reconciliation* explains the relational aspect of our salvation. The moment we receive Christ by faith, we enter into a personal relationship with Him. We are united with God in an eternal and inseparable bond (Rom. 8:38–39). We are bound in an indissoluble union with Him, as fellow heirs with Christ. The Holy Spirit has sealed us in that relationship, and we are absolutely secure in Christ.

The point of the cross is that through Christ's death and resurrection, we have become acceptable to God. This did not occur because God decided He could overlook our sin. It occurred because Christ forgave all of our sins so that He could present us to the Father, "holy, and blameless, and above reproach."

How would you describe what it means in this life to have a "relationship" with God through Jesus?

Jesus presents us to the Father, "holy, and blameless, and above reproach" (Col. 1:22). That is how God sees you through Jesus' eyes. What does it mean to you to be "holy, and blameless, and above reproach" before God?

What happened in the last twenty-four hours that has worked against your feeling "holy, and blameless, and above reproach"?

In what ways would you like to recognize God's presence in your life more fully?

TALK TO GOD

Father, when I understand how much You have done to invite me into a relationship with You, then I wonder how I could ever have the feelings of doubt, insecurity, and failure that I sometimes have. You cut right to the core with Your love for me. Yet the present-ness of this world and the values that seem inherent to a fallen human nature pull me away from resting in Your adoption of me. I confess that I still live sometimes like a stray pup instead of a prince when it comes to my spiritual understanding. I believe, but help my unbelief. Amen.

HOW MANY FINGERS ARE POINTING BACK AT YOU?

"Therefore the kingdom of heaven is like a certain king who wanted to settle accounts with his servants. And when he had begun to settle accounts, one was brought to him who owed him ten thousand talents. But as he was not able to pay, his master commanded that he be sold, with his wife and children and all that he had, and that payment be made. The servant therefore fell down before him, saying, 'Master, have patience with me, and I will pay you all.' Then the master of that servant was moved with compassion, released him, and forgave him the debt.

"But that servant went out and found one of his fellow servants who owed him a hundred denarii; and he laid hands on him and took him by the throat, saying, 'Pay me what you owe!' So his fellow servant fell down at his feet and begged him, saying, 'Have patience with me, and I will pay you all.' And he would not, but went and threw him into prison till he should pay the debt. So when his fellow servants saw what had been done, they were very grieved, and came and told their master all that had been done. Then his master, after he had called him, said to him, 'You wicked servant! I forgave you all that debt because you begged me. Should you not also have had compassion on your fellow servant, just as I had pity on you?' And his master was angry, and delivered him to the torturers until he should pay all that was due to him.

"So My heavenly Father also will do to you if each of you, from his heart, does not forgive his brother his trespasses."

—MATTHEW 18:23–35

PLAYING THE BLAME GAME

> **What connection do you see between how hard you are on yourself and how hard you are on others?**

Our perception of success and failure is often our primary basis for evaluating ourselves and others. If we believe that performance reflects one's value and that failure makes one unacceptable and unworthy of love, then we will usually feel completely justified in condemning those who fail, including ourselves. Self-condemnation may include name calling (*I'm so stupid! I can't do anything right!*), making self-deprecating jokes or statements, or simply never allowing any room for error in our performance.

We all tend to point an accusing finger, assigning blame for virtually every failure. Whenever we fail to receive approval for our performance, we are likely to search for a reason, a culprit, or a scapegoat. More often than not, we can find no one but ourselves to blame, so the accusing finger points right back at us. Self-condemnation is a severe form of punishment.

> **In the past twenty-four hours, what blame have you assessed to yourself?**

Why do you think it seems essential that someone be punished when something goes wrong?

If you aren't going to condemn yourself when you fail, what are the other options? What about when others fail?

In the story in Matthew 18:23–35, which character did you most relate to? Why?

TALK TO GOD

Father, when I condemn myself I place myself in Your role. Only You can know a person's heart, even mine. Only You can know a person's intentions, even my own. Only You can condemn, and only You can save. So I put my trust in You, not me. Let me receive Your mercy and offer it to those around me. I start by humbly saying thank You. Amen.

WHAT'S YOUR TRUE INHERITANCE?

For as many as are led by the Spirit of God, these are sons of God. For you did not receive the spirit of bondage again to fear, but you received the Spirit of adoption by whom we cry out, "Abba, Father." The Spirit Himself bears witness with our spirit that we are children of God, and if children, then heirs—heirs of God and joint heirs with Christ, if indeed we suffer with Him, that we may also be glorified together.

—ROMANS 8:14–17

BECOMING GOD'S CHILD

> **When you think about serving God, how do you picture yourself? As an employee? A servant? What image comes to mind?**

And for whom did Christ die? Was it for the saints who honored Him? Was it for a world that appreciated His sinless life and worshiped Him? No! Christ died for us, while we were in rebellion against Him. For while we were still helpless, Christ died for the ungodly at the right time.

Who can measure the fathomless depth of love that sent Christ to the cross? While we were the enemies of God, Christ averted the wrath we deserved so that we might become the sons of God.

Because we are His children, performance is no longer the basis of our worth. We are unconditionally and deeply loved by God, and we can live by faith in His grace. We were spiritually dead, but the Lord has made us alive and has given us the high status of sonship to the almighty God. It will take all of eternity to comprehend the wealth of His love and grace.

How does the fact that you are a child of God relate to your sense of worth?

How would you explain to someone else how being a child of God affects the very core of who you are?

Let your mind review the last twenty-four hours for a few minutes. Looking back, what evidence of God's Spirit can you see in yourself?

Your greatest need is to know that you matter. When you read through Romans 8:14–17, what stands out to you the most in regard to how you matter?

TALK TO GOD

God, You chose me when I didn't even recognize You. If I could take that in, I wouldn't spend my time pretending as if I could earn a place at Your table. Teach me how to honor my adoption by You. Teach me to live my life in the light of Your truth and grace. I will walk today in gratitude. Amen.

— *Day 18* —

CAN YOU OUTRUN THE PAST?

Remember my affliction and roaming, the wormwood and the gall. My soul still remembers and sinks within me. This I recall to my mind, therefore I have hope.

Through the LORD's mercies we are not consumed, because His compassions fail not. They are new every morning; great is Your faithfulness. "The LORD is my portion," says my soul, "therefore I hope in Him!"

The LORD is good to those who wait for Him, to the soul who seeks Him. It is good that one should hope and wait quietly for the salvation of the LORD.

— LAMENTATIONS 3:19–26

NEGOTIATING OLD GHOSTS

> **Looking back, what motivated you to want to work through your search for significance in a positive, proactive way?**

Too often our self-image rests solely on an evaluation of our past behavior, being measured only through a memory. Day after day, year after year, we tend to build our personalities upon the rubble of yesterday's personal disappointments.

Perhaps we find some strange kind of comfort in our personal failings. Perhaps there is some security in accepting ourselves as much less than we can become. That minimizes the risk of failure. Certainly, if we expect little from ourselves, we will seldom be disappointed!

But nothing forces us to remain in the mold of the past. By the grace and power of God, we can change! We can persevere and overcome! No one forces us to keep shifting our feet in the muck of old failures. We can dare to accept the challenge of building a new life.

What comes to mind when you think about the challenge of building a new life?

The great thing about God's mercies is that they are always available. There is a limitless supply of second, third, and fourth chances. Nobody but you is counting. What do you most want a second (or third or fourth) chance at?

Think about yesterday. Where do you most need to apply God's mercy so that you can move ahead with a clean slate?

What do you most hope will be different about your sense of significance as you look ahead to tomorrow, next week, or even next year?

TALK TO GOD

Father, because You know all things, You know how difficult it is for people to change their ways. I've spent years living, evaluating, deciding, and choosing to be where I am today. Some of this isn't working for me. I need Your help to change. Help me to see myself through Your eyes. Help me to believe in everything that is possible through You. Help me take a step back and really see the patterns in my life that lead to destruction instead of to Your abundant life. I know that's where You want to take me. Amen.

COULD YOU USE A "DO-OVER"?

For we ourselves were also once foolish, disobedient, deceived, serving various lusts and pleasures, living in malice and envy, hateful and hating one another. But when the kindness and the love of God our Savior toward man appeared, not by works of righteousness which we have done, but according to His mercy He saved us, through the washing of regeneration and renewing of the Holy Spirit, whom He poured out on us abundantly through Jesus Christ our Savior, that having been justified by His grace we should become heirs according to the hope of eternal life.

—TITUS 3:3–7

GETTING A (NEW) LIFE

> **If you could literally start over in your life (yes, given what you know now), what are some things you would do differently?**

Regeneration is not a self-improvement program, nor is it a cleanup campaign for our sinful natures. Regeneration is nothing less than the impartation of new life. Paul stated in Ephesians 2:5 that we were once dead in our sins, but we have since been made alive in Christ.

Regeneration is the renewing work of the Holy Spirit that literally makes each believer a new person at the moment trust is placed in Christ as Savior. In that wondrous, miraculous moment, we experience more than swapping one set of standards for another. We experience what Jesus called a new birth (John 3:3–6), a Spirit-wrought renewal of the human spirit, a transforming resuscitation that takes place so that the Spirit is alive within us (Rom. 8:10).

Resuscitation. Resuscitation happens when a person has stopped doing what he or she has to do to live—breathe. Someone breathes for that person to bring him or her back to life. What part of your life needs a breath of life from God today?

What, if anything, holds you back from allowing God to give you a new beginning?

Read through today's Scripture again. How would you describe
the role of the Holy Spirit in your day-to-day life?

Think back through the list you made for the opening
question. What ground would you recover? What relationships
could you improve even if you can't begin again? What early
callings in your life could you revisit? What changes in your
life would you like the Holy Spirit to participate with you in
exploring?

TALK TO GOD

Father God, life goes by so fast. It's easy to feel stuck, barely able to
rise to meet the moments, much less rise above them. Yet You say that I
can. You say that You have the power to create true change in me.
Teach me to access that power, to submit to Your process of
regeneration. I'm excited about the possibilities. Amen.

WHO THROWS THE FIRST STONE?

Then the scribes and Pharisees brought to Him a woman caught in adultery. And when they had set her in the midst, they said to Him, "Teacher, this woman was caught in adultery, in the very act. Now Moses, in the law, commanded us that such should be stoned. But what do You say?" This they said, testing Him, that they might have something of which to accuse Him. But Jesus stooped down and wrote on the ground with His finger, as though He did not hear.

So when they continued asking Him, He raised Himself up and said to them, "He who is without sin among you, let him throw a stone at her first." And again He stooped down and wrote on the ground. Then those who heard it, being convicted by their conscience, went out one by one, beginning with the oldest even to the last. And Jesus was left alone, and the woman standing in the midst. When Jesus had raised Himself up and saw no one but the woman, He said to her, "Woman, where are those accusers of yours? Has no one condemned you?"

She said, "No one, Lord."

And Jesus said to her, "Neither do I condemn you; go and sin no more."

—JOHN 8:3–11

FINDING FREEDOM FROM GUILT

> **What makes you feel guilty? What does guilt actually feel like inside of you? How does it affect you physically? Emotionally? How do you get over it?**

There is no burden that produces pain, fear, and alienation quite like the feeling of guilt. Many of us know it as a constant burden. Some of us respond to it like a whipped puppy, beaten down and ashamed. Some of us avoid it through the numbing effects of denial. Our association with guilt may be prompted by many factors: poor parental modeling of Christ's love and forgiveness, divorce, neglect, a particular past sin, and the emphasis some believers place on the "oughts" and "shoulds" of Christianity. Regardless of these influences, guilt need not be a way of life for us.

In Romans 8:1 Paul tells us, "There is therefore now no condemnation for those who are in Christ Jesus."

We feel we deserve condemnation, and we fail to realize that Christ has freed us from the guilt and condemnation our sins deserve.

What have you felt guilty about in the last twenty-four hours? If God doesn't want you to condemn yourself over those things, how do you think He would have you respond to them?

If God is not condemning you, not causing you to feel guilty, who (or what) are the influences in your life that prompt your guilt?

Read through the Scripture for today again. Why do you think it was the older people who walked away first from their opportunity to condemn the woman? How has your perspective on judging others changed as you have grown older? How about your perspective on judging yourself?

If Christ has freed us from guilt and condemnation, then we stand in a perpetual opportunity to begin again. Picture a train arriving at the station. You are standing with several extremely heavy bags of luggage. The train stops. "All aboard!" You take the first step and board the train, leaving your luggage behind on the platform. Everything you need will be provided on the journey. Those bags are the lies you've believed and the guilt you've carried. What specifically have you left behind? How does it feel to leave them behind?

TALK TO GOD

I have to wonder, Father, how many of my moments are spent feeling guilty about things You've already forgiven me for. Help me learn to move ahead in my life toward Your promises, rather than stay stuck in guilt. I realize that living in Your truth means living in the truth of Your forgiveness and redemption, not just in the reality of my sin. Sometimes I sit in the cage of guilt long after You've unlocked the door and opened it wide. I want to honor Your presence in my life by stepping into Your freedom. Help me to let the journey begin. Amen.

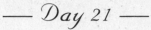

— *Day 21* —

WOULD YOU LIKE A NEW IDENTITY?

But you have not so learned Christ, if indeed you have heard Him and have been taught by Him, as the truth is in Jesus: that you put off, concerning your former conduct, the old man which grows corrupt according to the deceitful lusts, and be renewed in the spirit of your mind, and that you put on the new man which was created according to God, in true righteousness and holiness.

—EPHESIANS 4:20–24

RENEWING YOUR MIND

Our thoughts fly by at a record pace. It feels impossible to stop them long enough to change them, yet that has a lot to do with renewing our minds. How would you describe your thoughts toward yourself during the course of a difficult day? What do you mentally say to yourself as you weather the general difficulties of life?

What do I do now? I realize that I have bought into the satanic formulas. I recognize that my life has been affected by false beliefs. But I have believed this way all of my life. Is there any hope to break free from thought patterns I have held for so long?

It is hopeless for you to correct your thought process unless you cooperate with God to release His power in your mind. "And do not be conformed to this world, but be transformed by the renewing of your mind, so that you may prove what the will of God is, that which is good and acceptable and perfect" (Rom. 12:2 NASB).

"Renew your mind." But how do you do that? It is more than self-talk. It is more than repeating some words over and over. It is actually changing some of the thought patterns by which we have lived our entire lives.

Romans 12:2 talks about cooperating with God in renewing your mind. What does it mean to you to cooperate with God in changing your life?

Think back over the past several days. What signs can you see that you are more in touch with your own need for significance and more aware of how God is meeting that need?

Ephesians 4:20–24 mentions putting off the "old man" (your old way of thinking). What can you commit right now to putting off? What old patterns can you throw in a cardboard box and carry out to the curb?

Think about a difficult person whom you will face in the near future, someone who really pushes your buttons. These are the people who help us highlight the places in ourselves that could use some exploration. By changing old patterns, how will your response differ in your next encounter with this person?

TALK TO GOD

A new life—that would be a great thing, Father. That's what You offer me. Yet I'm comfortable with what is familiar to me even though I'd like to change. I need courage to follow You. Place that fire in me, God. Make me discontent enough to follow You into the unknown of Your renewal. Thank You for believing in a better life for Your creation, the life You had planned all along. Amen.

WHOSE MEASURE DO YOU MEASURE YOURSELF BY?

So then death is working in us, but life in you.

And since we have the same spirit of faith, according to what is written, "I believed and therefore I spoke," we also believe and therefore speak, knowing that He who raised up the Lord Jesus will also raise us up with Jesus, and will present us with you. For all things are for your sakes, that grace, having spread through the many, may cause thanksgiving to abound to the glory of God.

Therefore we do not lose heart. Even though our outward man is perishing, yet the inward man is being renewed day by day. For our light affliction, which is but for a moment, is working for us a far more exceeding and eternal weight of glory, while we do not look at the things which are seen, but at the things which are not seen. For the things which are seen are temporary, but the things which are not seen are eternal.

—2 CORINTHIANS 4:12–18

MEASURING UP

When you were growing up, what did you do that most often brought approval from the adults in your life?

Consciously or unconsciously, all of us have experienced this feeling that we must meet certain arbitrary standards to attain self-worth. Failure to do so threatens our security and significance. Such a threat, real or perceived, results in a fear of failure. At that point, we are accepting the false belief *I must meet certain standards to feel good about myself*. When we believe this about ourselves, Satan's distortion of truth is often reflected in our attitudes and behavior.

Because of our unique personalities, we each react very differently to this deception. Some of us respond by becoming slaves to perfection, driving ourselves incessantly toward attaining goals.

Now that you are grown, what does it seem that you most often do that wins the approval of the people around you?

How do the smiles on those people's faces relate to your value (or feelings of value) as a person?

How can you live in view of the smile of approval on God's face, instead of living as a slave to the approval of people around you?

How would you put into your own words the truth of what truly gives your life significance?

How driven are you in terms of ambition, accomplishment, and recognition from authorities and peers? What is a good balance for you?

TALK TO GOD

Father, I want to walk in Your truth, but lies are everywhere. They are in the culture around me, the misunderstandings I've grown up with, even sometimes in the messages I speak inside my own spirit. Reveal the lies to me, Father. Give me sight to see the difference between the darkness and the light. Let me live in view of the smile of approval on Your face, instead of as a slave to the approval of people around me who face just as many lies as I do. Thank You for Your love and acceptance. Amen.

WOULD YOU RATHER BE WEAK OR STRONG?

And He said to me, "My grace is sufficient for you, for My strength is made perfect in weakness." Therefore most gladly I will rather boast in my infirmities, that the power of Christ may rest upon me. Therefore I take pleasure in infirmities, in reproaches, in needs, in persecutions, in distresses, for Christ's sake. For when I am weak, then I am strong.

—2 CORINTHIANS 12:9–10

GETTING IT "RIGHT"

> Describe a time when everything worked right and you felt on top of your game.

As wonderful as it is to be pleasing to God, as much peace and joy as this would bring to our lives, what are our internal obstacles that keep us from reaching out and grasping this reality?

Our natural strengths will always fight against our dependence on God. It is painful to consider that we have a bit of pride about us. We may not even like to realize that we have been looking down on someone because we have outperformed them. But the fact is that there are times when we enjoy our success to the degree that we don't want to live our lives based on what God has done for us. We may even look down on those who have failed and consider ourselves above those failures.

What is so enticing about getting life right on your own, as opposed to getting life right through God's help?

Think about people whom you may, as much as you hate to admit it, look down on a little. How do you feel about the fact that God values them just as much as you? How do you feel about the fact that God doesn't love you any more because of what you have done or what you will do?

What are some of your natural strengths? In what ways might they be obstacles to depending on God for your sense of significance?

How do your weaknesses create opportunities for Christ's power to rest on you as 2 Corinthians 12:9–10 says?

Think about the moments that went right for you in the past day. Did those moments entice you to feel significant because you performed well or life went your way? What do you think is the balancing point between celebrating your victories and yet not depending on them to fill your soul?

Write a note to yourself, something you can read the next time you pick up this journal. Remind yourself that, succeed or fail, you are the same person with the same God who loves you. Make a note on tomorrow's entry to look back and read this message.

TALK TO GOD

Father, I'm so grateful for the abilities You've given me. I know, though, that I can't depend on these abilities as the foundation of my significance. Even talents and abilities can go away. Help me base my significance on the one thing that won't change—Your estimation of my life. Amen.

WHO TOLD YOU THAT YOU WERE LOVABLE?

"Take heed that you do not do your charitable deeds before men, to be seen by them. Otherwise you have no reward from your Father in heaven. Therefore, when you do a charitable deed, do not sound a trumpet before you as the hypocrites do in the synagogues and in the streets, that they may have glory from men. Assuredly, I say to you, they have their reward. But when you do a charitable deed, do not let your left hand know what your right hand is doing, that your charitable deed may be in secret; and your Father who sees in secret will Himself reward you openly.

"And when you pray, you shall not be like the hypocrites. For they love to pray standing in the synagogues and on the corners of the streets, that they may be seen by men. Assuredly, I say to you, they have their reward."

—MATTHEW 6:1–5

AIMING TO PLEASE

Do the good things that you do seem more powerful when someone else witnesses them? What satisfaction do you get from doing the right thing when no one is aware of it?

When we base our security on success and others' opinions, we become dependent on our abilities to perform and please others. We develop a *have-to* mentality: I *have to* do well on this exam. . . . I *have to* make that deal. . . . My father or mother *has to* appreciate me and be happy with my decisions.

Our self-esteem and view of God are usually a mirror of our parents' attitudes toward us. Our parents are our models of the character of God. When we do not have that fundamental sense of feeling lovable and protected by them, we tend to base our self-worth on how well we perform and please others instead of on what the sovereign God of the universe, our all-wise, omniscient Savior, says of us.

Is there anyone in your life right now whom you never seem able to please? Describe that relationship.

What are some of your beliefs about yourself that can be traced back to the people who loved you early on?

What do you think it takes to find a balance between honoring the presence of these significant people, and yet leaving behind some of their more negative influences?

Yesterday you were perhaps struggling through the source of your significance. Tomorrow you may still be struggling. Right now, in this moment, how would you describe the distance you've made so far in this journey?

TALK TO GOD

Father, even the people who should never let us down, do let us down sometimes. We are affected so deeply by the people who raised us. But Your love is surer than even those who brought us into the world. Help me see Your love, even in the midst of disappointing relationships. May You shine brightly in my life. Amen.

DO CREDENTIALS MEAN ANYTHING?

For when one says, "I am of Paul," and another, "I am of Apollos," are you not carnal?

Who then is Paul, and who is Apollos, but ministers through whom you believed, as the Lord gave to each one? I planted, Apollos watered, but God gave the increase. So then neither he who plants is anything, nor he who waters, but God who gives the increase. Now he who plants and he who waters are one, and each one will receive his own reward according to his own labor.

For we are God's fellow workers; you are God's field, you are God's building. According to the grace of God which was given to me, as a wise master builder I have laid the foundation, and another builds on it. But let each one take heed how he builds on it. For no other foundation can anyone lay than that which is laid, which is Jesus Christ.

—1 CORINTHIANS 3:4–11

LIVING AN AUTHENTIC LIFE

> Think about and write down some of those times in your life when you've found your worth and your identity in your group of friends rather than in what God says about you.

Because of reconciliation, we are completely acceptable *to* and *by* God. We enjoy a full and complete relationship with Him, and in this relationship, His determination of our value is not based on our performance. However, we may question what this relationship means as we attempt to apply it in our day-to-day experience.

Many of us are like the Christians at Corinth. We still try to obtain our significance the world's way, through success and approval. Often, we look only to other believers rather than to Christ Himself. We learn to use the right Christian words, claim divine power and guidance, and organize programs, and yet, so often, our spirituality lacks depth and substance. Our spiritual activities become human efforts lacking the real touch of the Master. In effect, we live a lie.

Why do we sometimes continue to do things that make us appear more spiritual than we actually are at the moment?

If, as you've read, God's concern is to make a home in us, to accept us, and then to live through us, what do we miss by living "a lie" spiritually?

Over the past twenty-four hours, what kinds of "Christian" things did you do out of a sense of duty? How do you think duty relates to discipline?

When you think of the balance between your actions being motivated by a deep conviction and connectedness to God and by a sense of duty, which one provides the most motivation in your life right now?

TALK TO GOD

Oh, Father, I want to live an authentic life before You. What good is it if I hide in the bushes, like Adam and Eve, because I am ashamed of who I am? What good is it especially if all the while You, in Your grace, have taken the responsibility to reconcile me to You? Thanks. I am so grateful for the reconciliation You've provided. Help me live in that gratitude. Amen.

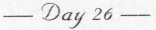

— *Day 26* —

WHOSE FAULT IS IT,
AFTER ALL?

Surely He has borne our griefs and carried our sorrows; yet we esteemed Him stricken, smitten by God, and afflicted. But He was wounded for our transgressions, He was bruised for our iniquities; the chastisement for our peace was upon Him, and by His stripes we are healed. All we like sheep have gone astray; we have turned, every one, to his own way; and the LORD has laid on Him the iniquity of us all.

—ISAIAH 53:4–6

TAKING THE BLAME

Take a moment to think about a conversation you've been a part of in which someone was trying to shift blame. How would you describe what's tough about taking the blame for something?

Whether our accusations are focused on ourselves or others, we all have a tendency to believe that someone has to take the blame.

Rather than being objective and looking for a solid, biblical solution to our problems, we often resort either to accusing someone else or to berating ourselves. Sometimes we blame others to make ourselves feel better.

In other situations, however, just the opposite is true. When a parent fails, a child often accepts the blame for that failure. Even as adults, we may readily assume blame in our relationships with those in authority.

Take a minute to think through your significant relationships. For the most part, do you tend toward absorbing blame or shifting it to someone else?

The truth is that God took all the blame so that you can move ahead in freedom and relief. What is it like to think about a relationship in which there is no blame?

If God has removed the blame through Christ, in what ways are you living a spiritually blame-free life?

Think of two pups. One has shied away with his tail tucked between his legs. The other is prancing around his master's feet. Where do you fit on the spectrum between those two images when you think about your relationship with God?

Close your eyes for a minute and think through some of the events of the last hours. What evidence of carrying blame in your life can you see?

TALK TO GOD

Father God, help me to see the issue of blame clearly in my life. I need to see where I blame myself for the wrongs others have done. I need to see where I have sloughed off the responsibility of facing life truthfully, all because I didn't want to receive any blame. Help me to look at life and at the people around me through the perspective of the blame You took on so that Your children could be blame-free, accepted, and unconditionally loved. Amen.

COULD YOU HAVE
SAVED YOURSELF?

But God, who is rich in mercy, because of His great love with which He loved us, even when we were dead in trespasses, made us alive together with Christ (by grace you have been saved), and raised us up together, and made us sit together in the heavenly places in Christ Jesus, that in the ages to come He might show the exceeding riches of His grace in His kindness toward us in Christ Jesus. For by grace you have been saved through faith, and that not of yourselves; it is the gift of God, not of works, lest anyone should boast.
—EPHESIANS 2:4–9

PAYING THE PRICE

Jesus Christ died as a sacrifice for your life. What does that sacrifice mean for you at this moment?

Propitiation means that Christ has satisfied the holy wrath of God through His payment for sin. There was only one reason for Him to do this: He loves us—infinitely, eternally, unconditionally, irrevocably, He loves us. God the Father loves us with the love of a father, reaching to snatch us from harm. God the Son loves us with the love of a brother, laying down His life for us. He alone has turned away God's wrath from us. There is nothing we can do, no amount of good deeds we can accomplish, and no religious ceremonies we can perform that can pay for our sins. Instead, Christ has conclusively paid for them so that we can escape eternal condemnation and experience His love and purposes both now and forever.

If the work is already done by God to open a relationship with you, where should your energy go in tending that relationship? How would you describe the kind of relationship you want to have with God?

If you aren't doing good deeds, being a good person, in order to win God's approval and acceptance (because you already have it), then what is your motivation?

How does this way of thinking relate to the typical do-good-get-good/do-bad-get-struck-by-lightning perspective?

Think about the last twenty-four hours for a moment. Try to focus on a couple of moments in which you felt valued and a couple in which you really didn't. Did those feelings of worth come from some outer influence? Did any of them come from your understanding of your relationship with God?

Write a short prayer expressing your gratitude for the work of Christ.

TALK TO GOD

Father, the foundation of my faith is the work of Christ. Thank You for that work. Thank You for becoming one of us to teach us to be like You. Thank You for loving us and wanting a relationship with us. The Cross and the Resurrection stand before me today as symbols of my worth in Your eyes. Let all the false sources of significance in my life fade away. Amen.

WHAT ARE YOU
HOLDING ON TO?

*Oh, give thanks to the LORD, for He is good! For His mercy
endures forever.*

*Let Israel now say, "His mercy endures forever." Let the house
of Aaron now say, "His mercy endures forever." Let those who fear
the LORD now say, "His mercy endures forever."*

*I called on the LORD in distress; the LORD answered me and set
me in a broad place. The LORD is on my side; I will not fear. What
can man do to me? The LORD is for me among those who help me;
therefore I shall see my desire on those who hate me. It is better to
trust in the LORD than to put confidence in man. It is better to trust
in the LORD than to put confidence in princes.*

—PSALM 118:1–9

LETTING GO AND HOLDING ON

Think about something you have to gear up for—a big
meeting, a family holiday, a pressure-filled week. What do you
do to give yourself confidence in facing the challenge ahead?

Dr. Paul Tournier once compared life to a man hanging from a trapeze. The trapeze bar was the man's security, his pattern of existence, his lifestyle. Then God swung another trapeze into the man's view, and he faced a perplexing dilemma. Should he relinquish his past? Should he reach for the new bar? The moment of truth came, Dr. Tournier explained, when the man realized that to grab the new bar, he must release the old one.

We may have difficulty relinquishing what is familiar (though painful) for what is unfamiliar because our fear of the unknown often seems stronger than the pain of a poor self-concept. It seems right to hang on. Any change in our behavior requires a release from our old self-concept, which is often founded in failure and the expectations of others. We need to learn how to relate to ourselves in a new way. To accomplish this, we must begin to base our self-worth on God's opinion of us and trust in His Spirit to accomplish change in our lives. Then, and only then, can we overcome Satan's deception that holds sway over our self-perception and behavior.

Describe a time when you had to let go of the familiar to learn or do something new with your life.

How does your life, or even the spiritual aspect of your life, compare to a trapeze act?

It's tough enough to change familiar patterns in our behavior. How much tougher, then, to make changes in our innermost being. Assess your own struggle in turning your back on the lifelong lies that you have held and instead believing that you are worthwhile.

Think back over the events and interactions that happened in the last twenty-four to forty-eight hours that are typical of your life and relationships, but that you would like to change in some way. How can you let go of those behaviors knowing what you know now?

TALK TO GOD

Some days, Father, I'm hanging on for dear life to what I know, what is familiar. Do I miss the trapezes You send my way? Help me be ready to jump when You offer me a new level of understanding You. Help me be ready to let go of what I think I need to in order to follow You into freedom and new life. Help me have a sense of what to hold on to and what to let go of. It's Your wisdom that I need. Thank You, Father. Amen.

WHICH RULES MAKE YOU NEW?

Therefore, if you died with Christ from the basic principles of the world, why, as though living in the world, do you subject yourselves to regulations—"Do not touch, do not taste, do not handle," which all concern things which perish with the using—according to the commandments and doctrines of men? These things indeed have an appearance of wisdom in self-imposed religion, false humility, and neglect of the body, but are of no value against the indulgence of the flesh.

If then you were raised with Christ, seek those things which are above, where Christ is, sitting at the right hand of God. Set your mind on things above, not on things on the earth.

—COLOSSIANS 2:20–3:2

MAKING YOU WHOLE

Think about your community, the people whom you live among, walk among, and value the opinions of (church, family, friends, work). What are the rules that make you a good person in that community? Particularly, what are the "don'ts" that really count?

Through the gift of God's grace, we are spiritually alive, forgiven, and complete in Him. Paul wrote the Colossian Christians: "For in Him [Christ] all the fullness of Deity dwells in bodily form, and in Him you have been made complete, and He is the head over all rule and authority" (Col. 2:9–10 NASB).

In the church at Colossae, false teachers taught that "completeness" came through a combination of philosophy, good works, other religions, *and* Christ. Paul's clear message was that we are made complete through Christ alone. To attempt to find completeness through any other source, including success, the approval of others, prestige, or appearance, is to be taken captive through philosophy and empty deception (Col. 2:8). Nothing can add to the death of Christ to pay for our sins and the resurrection of Christ to give us new life. We are complete because Christ has forgiven us and given us life and the capacity for growth and change.

What does it mean to you to be "complete"?

The Colossian church was not struggling with a philosophy that denied Christ. They were struggling with a philosophy that added to Christ. "Yes, Christ is the way. *And* you also need to do these things to be acceptable to God." Can you see evidence of this "heresy" anywhere in your life or community? What are the add-ons?

Yesterday you lived your life, made decisions, probably took care of a few people along the way, and negotiated choices along with many other things. How well do you think you did at tending your own soul in the midst of that?

You are almost at a halfway point in this journey. How well do you think you're doing at understanding where you find your significance?

TALK TO GOD

Complete. God, I want to be complete in You. I don't want to look to other things like my own righteousness, empty religion, even the love of friends and family to completely fill my soul. Only You can do that. But knowing the truth doesn't always make me live in the truth. Help me lay down the things that make me feel like I matter for the moment but don't really touch my soul. Help me depend on You for that. Amen.

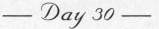

— *Day 30* —

WHAT'S THE POINT
OF GUILT, ANYWAY?

By this we know love, because He laid down His life for us. And we also ought to lay down our lives for the brethren. But whoever has this world's goods, and sees his brother in need, and shuts up his heart from him, how does the love of God abide in him?

My little children, let us not love in word or in tongue, but in deed and in truth. And by this we know that we are of the truth, and shall assure our hearts before Him. For if our heart condemns us, God is greater than our heart, and knows all things.

—1 JOHN 3:16–20

GETTING MOTIVATED

Think about times when you have been totally motivated to accomplish something. What were your greatest motivating factors?

Many of us have been told that we are still guilty even after we have trusted Christ to pay for our sins. And sadly, we have heard this in places that should be loudly and clearly proclaiming the forgiveness and freedom found in the Cross—our churches. Perhaps some people think that if they don't use guilt for motivation, we won't do anything. Guilt may motivate us for a short while until we adjust to being properly motivated. But a short period of waiting is well worth the long-term results of grace-oriented, intrinsic motivation.

Learn to identify incorrect teaching, guilt motivation, and the results of guilt in your own thoughts. Then refuse to believe the lies any longer, and focus instead on the unconditional love and forgiveness of Christ. His love is powerful, and He is worthy of our intense zeal to obey and honor Him. The result of proper motivation is an enduring, deepening commitment to Christ and His cause rather than the prevalent results of guilt motivation: resentment and the desire to escape.

Think about a time when you did something mostly out of guilt. How did you feel during that experience? After that experience?

In what ways was guilt a part of your religious or even just your emotional upbringing? How was guilt encouraged or discouraged in your faith or your home?

Who are the people who stir up the most guilt in you? Are they as good at it as they were a month ago? Are you as susceptible? How do you evaluate your progress in refusing to let your own sense of worth and value be affected by the guilt someone else would put on you?

Guilt is really a cheap shot kind of motivator. It's a shortcut to digging down in our souls and committing to following God at whatever cost. How would you describe your conviction of faith if guilt were completely out of the picture?

TALK TO GOD

It is my prayer, God, that You would live through me. I want to be boldly Yours. I want to be someone whom You don't just live in. I want to be someone whom You live through. Purify my heart and teach me to hear Your voice and live in the freedom of Your love. Amen.

WHO LEADS YOU THROUGH YOUR DARKEST JOURNEYS?

Now may the God of peace who brought up our Lord Jesus from the dead, that great Shepherd of the sheep, through the blood of the everlasting covenant, make you complete in every good work to do His will, working in you what is well pleasing in His sight, through Jesus Christ, to whom be glory forever and ever. Amen.

—HEBREWS 13:20–21

EXPLORING YOUR "SELF"

It takes some introspection to explore the foundation of your self-image, and it can be difficult. What do you find difficult about this process of self-exploration?

You should understand that you can do this on one of two levels. You can try to accomplish this by depending only on your natural mind, or you can seek God's guidance through the process. Doing The Trip In "naturally" can lead to some real bouts with depression, and you will come up with some very interesting information. However, you will not be experiencing God's power in this process.

If it is God who opens up an area to you, then you can be sure He is ready to heal that area. If it is just your mind going through rumination and introspection, then God may or may not intervene in a process that He did not start.

What areas of your life do you feel God leading you to explore?

Are there some problem areas of your past or your soul that you think may be relevant to your self-worth, but you don't feel God leading you there yet? Jot them down in simple words or phrases to refer back to later.

Self-exploration can often lead to bouts of depression. Has that been true for you, and under what circumstances? Why do you think looking into your soul can sometimes bring great sadness?

Take some time to think through the past twenty-four hours. How do you feel about yourself? In what ways are you giving yourself a break? In what specific ways do you feel a sense of value?

You are halfway through your 60-day journal. How do feel about the journey so far? What are your hopes for the remainder of the journey? Describe how you see God's role in this process with you.

TALK TO GOD

It's so easy to feel as if I'm doing life on my own. Father, too often life itself can distract me from an awareness of Your presence. But I want to walk through life with You. I know that is what You've called me to. So here I am, trying to explore my inner self, my motivations, my intentions in order to center my life on my relationship with You. Lead me in this search. Amen.

WHO ARE YOU WORKING FOR?

*Therefore I turned my heart and despaired of all the labor in which
I had toiled under the sun. For there is a man whose labor is with
wisdom, knowledge, and skill; yet he must leave his heritage to a
man who has not labored for it. This also is vanity and a great evil.
For what has man for all his labor, and for the striving of his heart
with which he has toiled under the sun? For all his days are
sorrowful, and his work burdensome; even in the night his heart
takes no rest. This also is vanity.*

*Nothing is better for a man than that he should eat and drink,
and that his soul should enjoy good in his labor. This also, I saw,
was from the hand of God.*

—ECCLESIASTES 2:20–24

MEETING EXPECTATIONS

**Do you consider yourself a high achiever? Do you feel driven
most of the time, or are you relaxed? Are you ambitious or
most often content right where you are? How would your
friends describe you?**

Many high achievers are driven beyond healthy limitations. Rarely
able to relax and enjoy life, they let their families and relationships

suffer as they strive to accomplish often unrealistic goals. On the other hand, the same false belief (*I must meet certain standards to feel good about myself*) that drives many to perfectionism sends others into a tailspin of despair. They rarely expect to achieve anything or to feel good about themselves. Because of their past failures, they are quick to interpret present failures as an accurate reflection of their worthlessness. Fearing more failure, they often become despondent and stop trying.

The pressure of having to meet self-imposed standards in order to feel good about ourselves can result in a rules-dominated life. Individuals caught in this trap often have a set of rules for most of life's situations, and they continually focus their attention on their performance and ability to adhere to their schedule.

What kind of goal setter are you? How realistic are the goals you set? How often do you accomplish your goals? When you don't, how does that affect you?

How closely do the goals you set for yourself relate to how you feel about yourself?

Think over the last day or two. Did accomplishing your goals ever take precedence over another person or even over your own well-being?

How would you evaluate yourself in terms of how well you separate your own sense of significance from your accomplishments?

TALK TO GOD

Father, I repent of sometimes caring more about measuring up to my own standards than even to Yours. Teach me to let go of what I think makes me OK, and instead help me hold on to Your grace. It feels so good to accomplish something, to win the respect and admiration of other people, to look good in the eyes of others. Help me to keep that in perspective. Even those good feelings can't heal my deepest wounds. Keep me coming back to You. Amen.

IF YOU COULD HAVE ONE THING . . . WHAT WOULD IT BE?

But what things were gain to me, these I have counted loss for Christ. Yet indeed I also count all things loss for the excellence of the knowledge of Christ Jesus my Lord, for whom I have suffered the loss of all things, and count them as rubbish, that I may gain Christ and be found in Him, not having my own righteousness, which is from the law, but that which is through faith in Christ, the righteousness which is from God by faith; that I may know Him and the power of His resurrection, and the fellowship of His sufferings, being conformed to His death, if, by any means, I may attain to the resurrection from the dead.

—PHILIPPIANS 3:7–11

MAINTAINING THE RIGHT RELATIONSHIP

What do you think is the most difficult or challenging thing about maintaining a relationship with God?

Some of us only know our faith as a series of rules or steps. In order for you to experience what Christ has provided through justification, you must receive it through your relationship with Him, not by performing some ritual.

Most of us have a priority system that goes something like this: air, water, food, control. We can hardly stand not to be in control. However, if we are going to base our worth on what Christ did for us, then we will sense a loss of control. This will be a greater struggle than you probably anticipate.

We will never achieve perfection on this earth, yet we are justified through Christ's righteousness. I am not minimizing the destructive nature of sin but simply trying to elevate our view of the results of Christ's payment on the cross. Understanding our complete forgiveness and acceptance before God gives us a greater desire to live for and serve God with joy.

In what ways do you find yourself caught in the "faith as a series of rules" pitfall? What makes that pitfall so enticing?

How do the words *religion* and *relationship* and *faith* fit together in your beliefs?

In Philippians 3:7–11 Paul is concluding a speech about his religious credentials. Before Paul became a Christian, he was a leader among Jews. Putting his faith in Jesus changed his priorities. How would you explain the difference between your religious credentials and your faith relationship with God?

Take a mental survey of the past week. Did your faith seem confined to church-related activities, or did your relationship with God permeate your life?

TALK TO GOD

There are good things in my life, Father—relationships, work, goals. I would be hard-pressed to say they don't matter. You created me in such a way that, of course, they do matter. But when I focus on You as the source of all those good things and, more than that, the source of my ability to live life fully among and through those things, then it all comes into perspective. In that sense, You are my One and Only. Help me to keep hold of that understanding. I honor Your place in my life as the one true source of significance. Amen.

DO YOU WATCH OUT FOR WHO'S WATCHING?

Then Jesus spoke to the multitudes and to His disciples, saying: "The scribes and the Pharisees sit in Moses' seat. Therefore whatever they tell you to observe, that observe and do, but do not do according to their works; for they say and do not do. For they bind heavy burdens, hard to bear, and lay them on men's shoulders; but they themselves will not move them with one of their fingers. But all their works they do to be seen by men. They make their phylacteries broad and enlarge the borders on their garments. They love the best places at the feasts, the best seats in the synagogues, greetings in the marketplaces, and to be called by men, 'Rabbi, Rabbi.' . . .

"But he who is greatest among you shall be your servant. And whoever exalts himself will be humbled, and he who humbles himself will be exalted."

—MATTHEW 23:1–7, 11–12

SEEKING TO BELONG

We can have many people who are important to us, but there are usually just a few who are so powerful in our lives that one word or even one tone of voice can completely knock us off balance. Who are those people in your life?

Our self-concept is determined not only by how we view ourselves but by how we think others perceive us. Basing our self-worth on what we believe others think of us causes us to become addicted to their approval.

We spend much of our time building relationships, striving to please people and win their respect. And yet, after all of our sincere, conscientious effort, it takes only one unappreciative word from someone to ruin our sense of self-worth. *I must be approved by certain others to feel good about myself.*

We are snared by this lie in many subtle ways. Believing it causes us to bow to peer pressure to gain approval. We may join clubs and organizations hoping to find a place of acceptance. We often identify ourselves with social groups to assure our acceptance and their approval. Many have admitted that experimentation with drugs or sex is a reaction to their need to belong.

How big a role does loneliness play in your life? How great is your need to belong?

In Matthew 6:1–6 Jesus gives some religious instructions. He says, in essence, that if you act out your faith merely to be seen as a person of faith, your actions are useless. There are parts of your faith that happen just between you and God. How much of your faith would you say is private, and how much happens in community? What is the balance?

How adept are you at relating to God in silent, private moments? Do those moments feel like authentic connections for you? What do you come away with from those moments?

How has your balance of quietness versus community fared over the past week? On which side of the equation do you need to make an adjustment?

TALK TO GOD

Father, as a child I watched the faces of those around me to know if I was safe, to know if I was right, to know if I was good. But now I need more than that. Now I need to sit alone with You and let You define for me that I am safe because You are right and You are good. It's easier to go with the rush of momentum around me. Help me be still before You so You can define our momentum together and so I will know Your place in my soul. Amen.

DOES WHAT YOU SAY MATCH WHAT YOU DO?

Nevertheless even among the rulers many believed in Him, but because of the Pharisees they did not confess Him, lest they should be put out of the synagogue; for they loved the praise of men more than the praise of God.

Then Jesus cried out and said, "He who believes in Me, believes not in Me but in Him who sent Me. And he who sees Me sees Him who sent Me. I have come as a light into the world, that whoever believes in Me should not abide in darkness. And if anyone hears My words and does not believe, I do not judge him; for I did not come to judge the world but to save the world."

—JOHN 12:42–47

SEEKING GOD'S APPROVAL

John 12:42–43 tells us a lot about the religious leadership of Jesus' day. Some of the religious leaders were afraid to admit they believed in Jesus because their peers would have rejected them. Even within the church, we hide our true selves in order to get the approval of other people. What beliefs or questions do you hold back for that same reason?

The desire for success and approval constitutes the basis of an addictive, worldly self-worth. Certainly, withdrawal from this dependency may cause us some pain as we change the basis of our self-worth, yet we will begin to discover true freedom and maturity in Christ only when we understand that our lives mean much more than what success or the approval of others can bring.

We can do nothing to contribute to Christ's free gift of salvation; furthermore, if we base our self-worth on the approval of others, then we are actually saying that our ability to please others is of greater value than Christ's payment.

Read that last sentence again. What thoughts and feelings does that bring to the surface?

At what point do you think your need for approval would be called an *addiction* to "worldly self-worth"?

Think back over the people you've talked to in the past twenty-four hours. Did you watch what you said with any of them? How much energy does walking-on-eggshells take in your social interactions? How does it leave you feeling?

Think about the people you will encounter tomorrow. Who will be the toughest person to talk to without trying to keep them happy? What perspective might help you be true to yourself in that conversation?

TALK TO GOD

Holy God, to live as if the approval of people matters more than Your approval really is an affront to Your presence in my life. I repent of that. Yet the patterns are now worn so deeply in me that I need Your help in learning that my worth is found only in You. Amen.

HOW DO YOU SAY THE COLD, HARD TRUTH?

Be angry, and do not sin. Meditate within your heart on your bed, and be still.

Offer the sacrifices of righteousness, and put your trust in the LORD.

There are many who say, "Who will show us any good?"

LORD, *lift up the light of Your countenance upon us. You have put gladness in my heart, more than in the season that their grain and wine increased. I will both lie down in peace, and sleep; for You alone, O* LORD, *make me dwell in safety.*

—PSALM 4:4–8

WALKING IN TRUTH

> **Think about times when you've expressed anger or resentment toward someone. What has been the typical response that you've received?**

There are appropriate and inappropriate ways of communicating our sense of anger or resentment to others, but these feelings need to be spoken, for their benefit and for ours. We also need to remember that learning how to express our feelings appropriately is a process. We can't expect to respond perfectly to everyone. It takes time to express years of repressed pain. It also takes time to learn how to respond firmly and clearly. Be patient with yourself. We have a choice in our response to failure: We can condemn or we can learn. All of us fail, but this doesn't mean that we are *failures*. We need to understand that failing can be a step toward maturity, not a permanent blot on our self-esteem. Like children first learning to walk, we all stumble and fall. And just like children, we can pick ourselves up and begin again.

When you know you are going to have a difficult conversation, how does it affect you? How do you prepare yourself mentally for it? Emotionally?

Resolving conflicts (which often goes along with difficult conversations) is a skill. The fact that our society is not good at it is evidenced by the number of lawyers and mediators we keep in business. How do you assess your ability to resolve conflicts?

The first step to relating to people honestly is to be sure of your own worth in God's eyes. When you are secure that you won't lose that, it's easier to be willing to make a few messes with people who will forgive you. What steps have you taken to relate to others honestly? What steps do you need to take?

Jot down a list of the people you need to have difficult conversations with. Pray about those people and conversations right now.

TALK TO GOD

Father, it is often far easier to say what I think someone wants to hear than it is to be truthful. That's part of this whole problem of finding my significance in other places and people. I want to win the approval of other people so I become less of me in order to fit their expectations. Instead, I should be true to You and to whom You have made me to be. But then the conversations can become less pleasant, less nice. Help me learn to be truthful, to be an authentic person, to be able to express my feelings. Amen.

IS THERE A FREE LUNCH?

But now in Christ Jesus you who once were far off have been brought near by the blood of Christ.

For He Himself is our peace, who has made both one, and has broken down the middle wall of separation, having abolished in His flesh the enmity, that is, the law of commandments contained in ordinances, so as to create in Himself one new man from the two, thus making peace, and that He might reconcile them both to God in one body through the cross, thereby putting to death the enmity. And He came and preached peace to you who were afar off and to those who were near. For through Him we both have access by one Spirit to the Father.

—EPHESIANS 2:13–18

MAKING PEACE

> Propitiation is a concept that has to do with making peace. The work of Christ made a way for peace between us and God. At this point in your life, in what ways do you feel like you're at peace with God? At peace with yourself?

There is nothing we can do, no number of good deeds we can accomplish, and no religious ceremonies we can perform that can pay for our sins. Instead, Christ has conclusively paid for them so that we can escape eternal condemnation and experience His love and purposes both now and forever.

Christ not only paid for our sins at one point in time but also continues to love us and teach us day after day. We have a weapon to use against Satan as he attacks us with doubts about God's love for us. Our weapon is the fact that Christ took our punishment upon Himself at Calvary. We no longer have to fear punishment for our sins, because Christ paid for them all—past, present, and future. This tremendous truth of propitiation clearly demonstrates that we are *truly and deeply loved by God*. His perfect love casts out all fear as we allow it to flood our hearts (1 John 4:18).

When have you experienced an attack from Satan? When have you struggled with doubts of God's love? How do you deal with those kinds of struggles?

We know the truth of Christ's sacrifice in our heads, but sometimes it doesn't reach our hearts. What typically short-circuits that connection for you?

Take a moment to think about the people whose love you feel most secure in. In what situations might you feel fearful in their presence? How much peace do you feel in their presence? Does God's love affect you in that way?

What areas of your life are you most at peace with right now? Which areas are causing you the most stress and fear? Take a few moments to invite God's peace into these places in your soul.

What did you fret over yesterday? What will be your greatest worry tomorrow? No matter what your answers to those questions, the core of you will still be loved and valued by God. Life might be difficult. You might experience unpleasantness and inconvenience, but you remain valued. Let that sink in. How does it affect your worries and fears?

TALK TO GOD

God of the ages, the fact that You would sacrifice Yourself for a relationship with me in the midst of my sin is no joking matter. That should change my perspective forever. Keep me from ignoring that truth of Your love. Speak loudly in my ear, and give me the awareness to listen to You. I worship You as God. I trust You as a good Father. I depend on You. Amen.

DO YOU HEAR FREEDOM CALLING?

Then Jesus said to those Jews who believed Him, "If you abide in My word, you are My disciples indeed. And you shall know the truth, and the truth shall make you free."

They answered Him, "We are Abraham's descendants, and have never been in bondage to anyone. How can you say, 'You will be made free'?"

Jesus answered them, "Most assuredly, I say to you, whoever commits sin is a slave of sin. And a slave does not abide in the house forever, but a son abides forever. Therefore if the Son makes you free, you shall be free indeed."

—JOHN 8:31–36

SURVIVING SHAME

> How would you compare the feelings of shame and guilt to a prison cell?

Shame usually results in guilt and self-depreciation, but it can also lead us to search for God and His answers. Our inner, undeniable need for personal significance was created to make us search for Him. He alone can fulfill our deep need. In Him, we find peace, acceptance, and love.

Through Him, we find the courage and power to develop into the men and women He intends us to be. Although Satan wants to convince us that we will always be prisoners of our failures and past experiences, by God's grace we can be freed from the guilt of our past and experience a renewed purpose for our lives.

Unhealthy shame is the feeling that you are broken and unfixable, that you are damaged. What kinds of circumstances or situations in your life make you feel that kind of shame?

Healthy shame is the knowledge that we are limited humans, broken in some ways just like everyone else. Healthy shame leads us to God. In what ways have your personal struggles (and even shame) drawn you to God?

How do you respond to the thought *Sin makes you its slave. God makes you His child?*

Describe a recent struggle with a past failure. Why is it so hard for you to let go and move on?

Most of us don't have to look far to find small failures, missteps, mistakes, and foolish judgments. Think about the past twenty-four hours. What failures, if any, did you experience? List some of them. How can you leave them with God right here and move ahead into this next day with your sense of worth intact? Mark through these failures as a symbol of your changed perspective.

TALK TO GOD

Father, help me find balance. Help me know my limitations without believing that they control my life more than You do. I don't want to spend my life unaware of my own shortcomings, but neither do I want to settle for less than what You have for me. The key is my trust in You and Your leadership. I know You will lead me well. Amen.

WHAT DIRECTION ARE YOU WALKING?

Therefore, putting away lying, "Let each one of you speak truth with his neighbor," for we are members of one another. "Be angry, and do not sin": do not let the sun go down on your wrath, nor give place to the devil. Let him who stole steal no longer, but rather let him labor, working with his hands what is good, that he may have something to give him who has need. Let no corrupt word proceed out of your mouth, but what is good for necessary edification, that it may impart grace to the hearers. And do not grieve the Holy Spirit of God, by whom you were sealed for the day of redemption. Let all bitterness, wrath, anger, clamor, and evil speaking be put away from you, with all malice. And be kind to one another, tenderhearted, forgiving one another, even as God in Christ forgave you.

Therefore be imitators of God as dear children.

—EPHESIANS 4:25–5:1

LIVING THE SPIRITUAL LIFE

Think back to when you became a Christian. (If you don't know exactly when it was, then think back to a time when you felt your faith move to a new level.) Describe that time in your life.

According to theologian Louis Berkhof, "Regeneration consists in the implanting of the principle of the new spiritual life in man, in a radical change of the governing disposition of the soul, which, under the influence of the Holy Spirit, gives birth to a life that moves in a Godward direction. In principle this change affects the whole man: the intellect . . . the will . . . and the feelings or emotion" (Louis Berkhof, *Systematic Theology*, Grand Rapids: Eerdmans, 1941, 468).

When we trust Christ and experience new life, forgiveness, and love, our lives will begin to change. Still, regeneration does not effect an instantaneous change in the full realm of our performance. We will continue to stumble and fall at times, but the Scriptures clearly instruct us to choose to act in ways that reflect our new lives and values in Christ.

What evidence of spiritual life do you see in yourself? Conviction of sin? A desire to be closer to God? A discontentment with the same old stuff?

No matter where you are in your spiritual walk, you can turn toward God and start moving closer. In what ways would you like to be closer to God? What are you discontented with spiritually in your life?

Read through the signs of spiritual life listed in Ephesians 4:25–5:1. Which ones sparked a response as you read them? How would you like to see these incorporated more into your life?

Review your conversations, interactions, and quiet moments in the past twenty-four hours. In what areas did you see signs of God's regeneration? How would you like to see new life more obvious in the way you live each day?

TALK TO GOD

God, I've been thinking a lot about the changes I need to make. Gradually I'm understanding how to listen to the truth of Your voice instead of the lies and myths that I've learned along the way. Help me today to start walking in truth in a whole new way. Help me to hit a growth spurt that takes me to a new level of following You. I want to feel new life bubbling to the surface. I want to please You. Amen.

HAVE YOU LOOKED AT THE WILL YET?

Blessed be the God and Father of our Lord Jesus Christ, who has blessed us with every spiritual blessing in the heavenly places in Christ, just as He chose us in Him before the foundation of the world, that we should be holy and without blame before Him in love, having predestined us to adoption as sons by Jesus Christ to Himself, according to the good pleasure of His will, to the praise of the glory of His grace, by which He made us accepted in the Beloved.

In Him we have redemption through His blood, the forgiveness of sins, according to the riches of His grace which He made to abound toward us in all wisdom and prudence, having made known to us the mystery of His will, according to His good pleasure which He purposed in Himself. . . .

In Him you also trusted, after you heard the word of truth, the gospel of your salvation; in whom also, having believed, you were sealed with the Holy Spirit of promise, who is the guarantee of our inheritance until the redemption of the purchased possession, to the praise of His glory.

—EPHESIANS 1:3–9, 13–14

ACCEPTING OUR SPIRITUAL INHERITANCE

How do you view your faith most frequently—as something you have to keep going, or as something that keeps you going?

Many of us are hindered in our walk with God because we do not realize the nature and depth of the love and power available to us in Christ. We haven't yet fully comprehended the magnificent truths of the Scriptures—that we are deeply loved, totally forgiven, fully pleasing, totally accepted, and complete in Christ, with all the power of His resurrection available to us. We may be like the West Texas sheep rancher who lived in poverty even though vast resources of oil were under his property. He was fabulously rich but didn't even know it. Since its discovery many years ago, this oil field has proven to be one of the richest and most productive in the world. Similarly, we have incredible resources available to us through the Holy Spirit, who enables us to experience the reality of Christ's love and power in many ways.

What are the hidden riches in your life?

Read Ephesians 1:3–9, 13–14 for a description of your spiritual inheritance. Write down the phrases that touch your heart or make you feel excited.

When we feel a sense of significance, we can share with other people out of our fullness, instead of trying to fill our emptiness. When you consider your spiritual inheritance, are you left with a feeling of spiritual abundance, or do you still feel emptiness?

Some people "talk poor" even though they have money. Some Christians live poor, even though they have eternity. Think about the past twenty-four hours. In what ways did you live like a child of the King?

TALK TO GOD

It's amazing, Lord, that You call me Your child, yet I live sometimes like a spiritual pauper. Why don't I take You at Your word? Do I forget? Does the truth get mentally crowded out? You've asked me to stake a claim in Your kingdom. Teach me to do that. Teach me to approach life as a member of a royal family. Amen.

WHAT DOES LIFE SQUEEZE OUT OF YOU?

Therefore lay aside all filthiness and overflow of wickedness, and receive with meekness the implanted word, which is able to save your souls.

But be doers of the word, and not hearers only, deceiving yourselves. For if anyone is a hearer of the word and not a doer, he is like a man observing his natural face in a mirror; for he observes himself, goes away, and immediately forgets what kind of man he was. But he who looks into the perfect law of liberty and continues in it, and is not a forgetful hearer but a doer of the work, this one will be blessed in what he does.

If anyone among you thinks he is religious, and does not bridle his tongue but deceives his own heart, this one's religion is useless.

—JAMES 1:21–26

LEARNING UNDER PRESSURE

You probably are familiar with the concept of GIGO—"Garbage In, Garbage Out." Explain how that phrase applies to false beliefs.

Situations trigger false beliefs. In those situations there are almost always individuals whom we blame for our emotions.

The next time you become upset and blame someone for your response, think about your tube of toothpaste. This morning you squeezed your toothpaste tube, and out of it came toothpaste. The reason the toothpaste came out is because that is what is in the tube. Someone may have squeezed you once, and out of you may have come responses that were really ungodly, maybe even embarrassing. You blame another for your responses, but you have to understand that what came out of you is what was in you. Often God allows us to undergo troubling circumstances so that we can see what is inside of us.

Think about the troubling circumstances you've faced in the past twenty-four hours. What did they reveal about you?

Think about the difficult people you've interacted with over the past twenty-four hours. What did it seem like they *made* you feel?

When you get upset when someone is unhappy with you, what inner belief does that reveal in you?

Some people (possibly yourself!) believe that if they did everything perfectly, nothing would go wrong. Based on what you know, how would you adjust that statement to reflect what you really believe about life?

If you were going to write a "Real-Life Manual on Personal Significance" and the publisher asked you to write a one-sentence synopsis of the book, what would it be?

TALK TO GOD

Father God, during the next twenty-four hours I will encounter many situations. Help me gain from them what You have for me to learn. Teach me about myself through the pressures I face. Prepare me to be a better person, to be more like You, through the events of this next day. You are the source of my sense of worth. Amen.

— *Day 42* —

WHAT ARE THE EFFECTS OF FAILURE?

The steps of a good man are ordered by the LORD, *and He delights in his way. Though he fall, he shall not be utterly cast down; for the* LORD *upholds him with His hand.*

I have been young, and now am old; yet I have not seen the righteous forsaken, nor his descendants begging bread. He is ever merciful, and lends; and his descendants are blessed.

—PSALM 37:23–26

FACING FAILURE AND SUCCESS

> In Psalm 37 David states that though a good man may fall, he shall not be "utterly cast down." How would you describe the difference between falling and being utterly cast down?

For many of us, life is like walking through a very dark house with no lights for illumination. You may not know when you're going to trip over the next object, but reason tells you it may be very soon. The same is true with failure. There is no way to escape the experience of failure. If that experience reduces your sense of value, then with the failure will come pain. The next time you experience anxiety, ask yourself what failure you sense may be about to occur.

When we base our self-worth on our performance and are successful, we often develop an inflated view of ourselves that leads to pride. However, this sense of self-esteem lasts only until our next failure (or risk of failure).

Through this journal, you have visited the issue of failure several times. At this point, how would you gauge your fear of failure? Is it intense? Does it hamper you from living life the way you want to?

Have you found that place in yourself where you can distinguish the difference between God's approval and people's approval?

Name three things that would be worse than failing in front of people whose opinions are important to you.

What's on your agenda tomorrow that will require some kind of risk of failure? Based on what you know about God and His relationship to you, how can you prepare for it?

TALK TO GOD

Father, teach me through my failures. I think of the things that cause me to feel that I've failed and I give them to You. Use them as tools in my life. Help me to face life aware of the chance that I might fail yet ready to follow You at any cost. Amen.

DO YOU NEED
VISION CORRECTION?

What then shall we say to these things? If God is for us, who can be against us? He who did not spare His own Son, but delivered Him up for us all, how shall He not with Him also freely give us all things? Who shall bring a charge against God's elect? It is God who justifies. Who is he who condemns? It is Christ who died, and furthermore is also risen, who is even at the right hand of God, who also makes intercession for us. Who shall separate us from the love of Christ? Shall tribulation, or distress, or persecution, or famine, or nakedness, or peril, or sword? As it is written:

> *"For Your sake we are killed all day long;*
> *We are accounted as sheep for the slaughter."*

Yet in all these things we are more than conquerors through Him who loved us. For I am persuaded that neither death nor life, nor angels nor principalities nor powers, nor things present nor things to come, nor height nor depth, nor any other created thing, shall be able to separate us from the love of God which is in Christ Jesus our Lord.

— ROMANS 8:31–39

SEEING GOD CLEARLY

How would you describe God to someone who has never heard anything about Him?

The love of God and His acceptance of us are based on grace, His unmerited favor. They are not based on our ability to impress God through our good deeds.

We love because He first loved us. Understanding this will highly motivate us.

This great motivating factor is missing in many of our lives because we don't really believe that God loves us unconditionally. We expect His love to be conditional, based on our ability to earn it. Our experience of God's love is based on our perception. If we believe that He is demanding or aloof, we will not be able to receive His love and tenderness. Instead, we will be either afraid of Him or angry with Him. Faulty perceptions of God often prompt us to rebel against Him. Our image of God is the foundation for all of our motivations.

"Our image of God is the foundation for all of our motivations." What is your image of God? How does that affect your motivations?

Take a few quiet moments to think about God's love and commitment to you. Don't think about what you *should* believe. Ask God to reveal your true beliefs about His love. What comes to mind?

There is no truer indicator of our view of God than our own sense of significance. How could we feel insignificant if we understand the lengths to which God has gone to have a relationship with us? How would you describe the lengths to which God has gone to have a relationship with you?

What false beliefs about God have been revealed to you through this journey?

TALK TO GOD

Father, help me to see You. Help me to see past the false images of You that have been set up in my soul through wounds, misunderstandings, and immaturity. If I could see You as You are, I would know Your love for me. Knowing that love in its sincerity would touch the bottom of my soul and would allow me to touch others in a whole new way. Help me see You. Amen.

TOGETHER OR ALONE?

There is one alone, without companion: He has neither son nor brother. Yet there is no end to all his labors, nor is his eye satisfied with riches. But he never asks, "For whom do I toil and deprive myself of good?" This also is vanity and a grave misfortune.

Two are better than one, because they have a good reward for their labor. For if they fall, one will lift up his companion. But woe to him who is alone when he falls, for he has no one to help him up. Again, if two lie down together, they will keep warm; but how can one be warm alone? Though one may be overpowered by another, two can withstand him. And a threefold cord is not quickly broken.

—ECCLESIASTES 4:8–12

LOVING EACH OTHER

> **What are the advantages and disadvantages to going it alone on a particular project? How about life in general?**

Another symptom of our fear of rejection is our inability to give and receive love. We find it difficult to open up and revel our inner thoughts and motives because we believe that others will reject us if they know what we are really like. Therefore, our fear of rejection leads us to superficial relationships or isolation.

The fear of rejection is rampant, and loneliness is one of the most dangerous and widespread problems in America today. Ninety-two percent of the Christians attending a recent Bible conference admitted in a survey that feelings of loneliness are a major problem in their lives. This is a tragic commentary on the people about whom Christ said, "By this all men will know that you are My disciples, if you have love for one another" (John 13:35 NASB).

To what degree do you feel lonely?

In what situations has a fear of rejection led to loneliness in your own life?

Reflect on your schedule yesterday. At any point did you feel lonely or isolated? In other words, did you have any moments when you longed for a sense of connection that just wasn't there?

God created us to need people. There is no sin in that. But the truth is that there are certain kinds of loneliness that only God can meet. People cannot completely fill us. Think of the people closest to you. How would you describe the places in you that even they can't touch?

We have to be alone sometimes. Spouses die or are an emotional no-show. Children grow up and move away. Loved ones leave us. If we don't connect with God in a foundational kind of way, then when people leave us, we will feel utterly alone. That's not reality, though. Close your eyes and imagine yourself in a deserted place. Feel God's presence there with you. Describe that feeling.

TALK TO GOD

Father God, it's sometimes easier to reach out for a person's hand to hold than to reach out to You spiritually. Teach me to sense Your presence. Help me to open myself up to people whom You bring into my life. I know You'll touch me through them. Teach me, though, not to try to make them be a replacement for You. Amen.

WHO ARE WE TOGETHER?

Be kindly affectionate to one another with brotherly love, in honor giving preference to one another; not lagging in diligence, fervent in spirit, serving the Lord; rejoicing in hope, patient in tribulation, continuing steadfastly in prayer; distributing to the needs of the saints, given to hospitality.

Bless those who persecute you; bless and do not curse. Rejoice with those who rejoice, and weep with those who weep. Be of the same mind toward one another. Do not set your mind on high things, but associate with the humble. Do not be wise in your own opinion.

Repay no one evil for evil. Have regard for good things in the sight of all men. If it is possible, as much as depends on you, live peaceably with all men.

—ROMANS 12:10–18

FINDING HEALING

> **Parents can only give what they have themselves. In what ways did your parents pass along a sense of significance to you?**

The poorer the parental modeling of God's love, forgiveness, and power, the greater our difficulty in experiencing and applying these characteristics in our lives. Instead of being refreshed by the truth of

God's love, if we have been deeply wounded, we may recoil from it, believing that we are unlovable. We may be fearful of reaching out and being hurt again. Whatever the cause, the result is withdrawal from the very idea of being loved and accepted.

Those who have received poor parental modeling need new models—loving Christian friends to experience the love and grace of God. Through His body of believers, God often provides us with models of His love so that our perception of His character can be slowly reshaped into one that is more accurate, resulting in a healthier relationship with Him. Then our deep emotional, spiritual, and relational wounds can begin to heal, and we can more fully experience God's unconditional love.

Make a list of the people God has brought into your life who have revealed His love to you.

Imagine a scale of emotional woundedness. On one end are a few nicks and cuts. On the other end are wounds that remind you of a soldier dragged off the battlefield during a skirmish. Where do you fit on that spectrum? Describe the extent of the emotional and spiritual woundedness that you have experienced in life.

What will it take to heal your emotional wounds? Your spiritual ones?

Sit still for a few minutes and invite God to comfort and heal your wounds from past hurts and disappointments. Think about God gently soothing your pain the way a good dad would take care of his hurt child. In what ways do you struggle with believing that God will heal you?

Why do you think ignoring our spiritual wounds won't make them go away?

TALK TO GOD

Father, You know each childhood scar I received, physically and emotionally. You were there. Help me identify any areas in my life that are still wounded. Help me to see the people whom You have sent to me to bring Your healing. Help me not to live in a dark place unable to see Your light guiding me. Amen.

WHO'S THE HARDEST ONE TO LET OFF THE HOOK?

*Seeing then that we have a great High Priest who has passed through
the heavens, Jesus the Son of God, let us hold fast our confession.
For we do not have a High Priest who cannot sympathize with our
weaknesses, but was in all points tempted as we are, yet without sin.
Let us therefore come boldly to the throne of grace, that we may
obtain mercy and find grace to help in time of need.*

—HEBREWS 4:14–16

FORGIVING YOURSELF

One of the main points of Hebrews 4:14–16 is that Jesus truly
understands how hard it is at times to be human. He knows
the temptations of power and pride and lust. He knows what it
is to be rejected. He knows what it is to be misunderstood and
disapproved of. How does knowing that about Jesus affect you?

If we have trusted Christ for our salvation, God has forgiven us and
wants us to experience His forgiveness on a daily basis. Moses was a
murderer, but God forgave him and used him to deliver Israel from
Egypt. David was an adulterer and a murderer, but God forgave him
and made him a great king. Peter denied the Lord, but God forgave

him, and Peter became a leader in the church. God rejoices when His children learn to accept His forgiveness, pick themselves up, and walk after they have stumbled. But we must also learn to forgive ourselves.

Think about the fact that so many of the great leaders of the Bible failed spiritually at times: Moses, David, and Peter are among many who fit that profile. What does that mean for you?

How are you at forgiving yourself? How does your ability to forgive yourself compare to God's willingness to forgive you?

Think back over the past twenty-four hours. What is the one thing you did that remains difficult to move on from? Write yourself a note of forgiveness. Be as kind and respectful as you would be to someone else. Read it aloud.

Mistakes, even sins, don't change who we are. We were never perfect to begin with. Since we've received God's approval even in our imperfect state, in what ways should our mistakes and failures affect us?

Put into words the false belief that we hold if we think we are less valued as humans because we fail sometimes.

TALK TO GOD

Father God, it is sometimes hard to face my own imperfections. I would rather always be strong, always be helpful, always be gracious. But I'm not. Sometimes I'm needy, selfish, or petty. Help me to understand that Your love surpasses all that. Help me remember that You sought out a relationship with me knowing full well my sinfulness. Help me see my own weakness and gratefully accept Your love. Amen.

WHO WILL MAKE IT RIGHT?

But if we walk in the light as He is in the light, we have fellowship with one another, and the blood of Jesus Christ His Son cleanses us from all sin.

If we say that we have no sin, we deceive ourselves, and the truth is not in us. If we confess our sins, He is faithful and just to forgive us our sins and to cleanse us from all unrighteousness. If we say that we have not sinned, we make Him a liar, and His word is not in us.

My little children, these things I write to you, so that you may not sin. And if anyone sins, we have an Advocate with the Father, Jesus Christ the righteous. And He Himself is the propitiation for our sins, and not for ours only but also for the whole world.

—1 JOHN 1:7–2:2

WALKING IN THE LIGHT

> How do you know when you are "walking in the light"? What is the difference, in your experience, between walking in the light and walking in the darkness? How does it actually feel different?

How do we begin to experience freedom from Satan's lie *Those who fail are unworthy of love and deserve to be punished?* We will be increasingly freed as we understand and apply the truth of propitiation in the context of loving and supportive relationships, where we can express ourselves honestly and receive both the warmth of affirmation and the challenge of God's Word.

The Scriptures indicate that Satan accuses believers of being unworthy of God's grace. It is his desire that we cower under the fear of punishment.

How are we to overcome Satan, the accuser, and experience our acceptance in Christ? There is only one way: by the sacrificial blood of Christ on the cross, the blood of the Lamb. To do this, we must first stop trying to overcome our feelings of condemnation and failure by penitent actions. Defending ourselves or trying to pay for our sins by our actions leads only to a guilt-and-penance spiral because we can never do enough on our own to justify our sins.

Think about the phrase "a guilt-and-penance spiral." What experiences come to mind from your past? What about from this last week?

Since Satan is the accuser, we can safely assume that none of the accusing, taunting voices we hear are from God. While the Spirit of God does convict us of sin, He doesn't do it accusingly. If you stopped listening to any accusing voice, including your own, how would that cut down on the negativity that you have to battle on a day-to-day basis?

What does it mean to you that Jesus functions as your Advocate before God according to 1 John 1:7–2:2?

Imagine an accusing voice in your head. You know the kind— "How could you *do* that?!?" Now imagine Jesus standing up for you. What would Jesus say to that voice?

TALK TO GOD

Father, I know You want my repentance but not my groveling. I know You want me to come to You as Your loved child and not as a fearful servant. I know that You want me to confess my sins to You but not condemn myself for them. Help me to live out these truths and to honor You with my understanding of You. Amen.

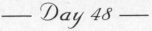

ARE YOU ASHAMED?

Have mercy upon me, O God, according to Your lovingkindness;
according to the multitude of Your tender mercies, blot out my
transgressions. Wash me thoroughly from my iniquity, and cleanse
me from my sin.

For I acknowledge my transgressions, and my sin is always
before me. Against You, You only, have I sinned, and done this evil
in Your sight—that You may be found just when You speak, and
blameless when You judge.

Behold, I was brought forth in iniquity, and in sin my mother
conceived me. Behold, You desire truth in the inward parts, and in
the hidden part You will make me to know wisdom.

—PSALM 51:1–6

FEELING INFERIOR

According to Psalm 51:1–6, God desires truth in the "inward parts" of us. We think of truth in terms of what we say and do. But honesty with ourselves and before God is where a life of integrity begins. How authentic do you think you are in God's presence?

By definition, shame is a deep sense of inferiority. Feelings of inferiority can result from prolonged patterns of failure, or they can stem from only one or two haunting instances. Either way, they can destroy our self-worth and, as a result, adversely affect our emotions and behavior. These perceptions of ourselves aren't easily altered.

We often behave in a manner that is consistent with our perception of ourselves. Shame often prompts us to view ourselves as victims. Some of us try to compensate for gnawing feelings of shame through passivity, refusing to invest any part of ourselves in relationships and responsibilities. Some of us develop facades. We are often afraid that if people really knew us, we would again experience hurt and rejection.

In what ways do you feel that you are inferior to people whom you meet (even if you know in your head it's not true)?

"Gnawing feelings of shame" is an apt description. When we carry shame with us, wondering why we don't seem OK like everyone else (seems to be), there is a constant gnawing on our souls. We can get used to it, like the sound of air conditioning or other background noise. Quiet yourself for a few minutes and listen. Ask God to reveal your feelings of shame. What comes to mind?

Take another minute and think about the past twenty-four hours. When did you feel a sense of not measuring up? Jot down some words or phrases to identify those times.

While you may have felt as though you didn't measure up during those times, the fact is that your feelings have nothing to do with your worth as a person. Your worth is based on something entirely different than your feelings or the careless words (looks, thoughts) of others. If you could go back and whisper in your own ear at those difficult moments yesterday, what would you say?

A new day lies before you. How can you prepare yourself with a sense of worth to face this day?

TALK TO GOD

God, I confess that I am afraid. I confess my fears of not measuring up. I confess my fears of not really being loved if I were really known. I confess that I don't always walk with my head held high in Your grace. Heal me. Teach me. I will follow You. Amen.

DO YOU KNOW WHOSE YOU ARE?

But when the fullness of the time had come, God sent forth His Son, born of a woman, born under the law, to redeem those who were under the law, that we might receive the adoption as sons.

And because you are sons, God has sent forth the Spirit of His Son into your hearts, crying out, "Abba, Father!" Therefore you are no longer a slave but a son, and if a son, then an heir of God through Christ.

—GALATIANS 4:4–7

BELONGING TO GOD

What does it mean to you, in practical terms, that you are a child of God?

We are to put on, or envelop ourselves in, this new self that progressively expresses Christian character in our attitudes and behavior. We are marvelously unique, created to reflect the character of Christ through our individual personalities and behavior. In a different and special way, each believer has the capability to shine forth the light of God. No two will reflect light in exactly the same way.

The truth of regeneration can dispel the specter of the past. Our sins have been forgiven, and we now have tremendous capabilities for growth and change because we are new people with the Spirit of God living in us. Yes, when we sin we will experience its destructive effects and the Father's discipline, but our sin will never change the truth of who we are in Christ.

How would you describe the "destructive effects" of sin in your life?

We all have behaviors that snag us along the way. Describe some of the typical snags that you face, particularly in your interactions with other people.

Galatians 4:4–7 compares slaves to sons. Think about your general spiritual outlook in your unguarded moments. Where would you fit on the spectrum between slaves and sons, not in reality, but in the way you perceive yourself before God?

Glance over your schedule for the next day. What challenges
are there? What situations will require you to rise to the
occasion? How can you see these as an opportunity to "shine
forth the light of God" in your own distinctive way?

Think of the difference between Cinderella as a stepchild
scullery maid and Cinderella as a princess on a magical night.
God offers us the magical part. What will it take for you to
believe?

TALK TO GOD

Abba Father, why do I live like a slave instead of Your child? Why do I
ever hide from You? Why do I ever live life as a drudgery when every
day You are making me new? Teach me to connect with You. Amen.

WHAT DOES IT MEAN TO BE REDEEMED?

But also for this very reason, giving all diligence, add to your faith virtue, to virtue knowledge, to knowledge self-control, to self-control perseverance, to perseverance godliness, to godliness brotherly kindness, and to brotherly kindness love. For if these things are yours and abound, you will be neither barren nor unfruitful in the knowledge of our Lord Jesus Christ. For he who lacks these things is shortsighted, even to blindness, and has forgotten that he was cleansed from his old sins.

Therefore, brethren, be even more diligent to make your call and election sure, for if you do these things you will never stumble; for so an entrance will be supplied to you abundantly into the everlasting kingdom of our Lord and Savior Jesus Christ.

—2 PETER 1:5–11

LIVING REDEEMED

> How is your significance meter running? What evidence is there in your life that you've tapped into God's love and acceptance of you?

Now redeemed, our rightful purpose to rule in life will only be denied if we continue to allow Satan to deceive us. If we fail to recognize our true position of worship and to exercise our new power and authority, we will remain trapped in the world's system. Satan's lies and schemes are designed to keep us from recognizing and experiencing these wonderful truths.

In order to overcome Satan's lies and begin to enjoy freedom from false beliefs, we need to have a clear understanding of what Christ has done for us through His death on the cross. The more fully we understand the implications of Christ's sacrifice, the more we will experience the freedom, motivation, and power God intends for us. God's Word is the source of truth: the truth about Christ, the cross, and redemption.

"Freedom, motivation, and power." That is what should come from understanding Christ's sacrifice for us. In what ways have you experienced the freedom, motivation, and power that comes from Christ's sacrifice?

In what ways do you still feel "trapped in the world's system"?

You've read a lot during these last weeks about the lies that you believe and about the lies that Satan promotes. What are the lies that still keep you blinded to the power you should receive from being God's redeemed?

In 2 Peter 1:5–11 you read that the person who has no evidence of faith, virtue, self-control, perseverance, godliness, and kindness is shortsighted—even blind—and has "forgotten that he was cleansed from his old sins." What tends to make you forget that you have been cleansed from sin?

Think back over the past twenty-four hours. Jot down some ways that you experienced God's presence.

TALK TO GOD

Father, I don't want to forget the gifts that come to me because of our relationship. I don't want to hurry past You on the way to the daily, menial details of life. Thank You for calling me back, taking away my blindness, helping me remember. Thank You for creating me worthy of love. Amen.

HOW MANY DIE-HARD FANS DO YOU HAVE?

Grace to you and peace from God our Father and the Lord Jesus Christ.

I thank my God upon every remembrance of you, always in every prayer of mine making request for you all with joy, for your fellowship in the gospel from the first day until now, being confident of this very thing, that He who has begun a good work in you will complete it until the day of Jesus Christ.

—PHILIPPIANS 1:2–6

GROWING SPIRITUALLY

> **In what ways do you feel confident that God will complete the work He has begun in you? On what do you base your confidence?**

The Father is busy in our lives even when we are unaware of His activities. He wants us to find freedom in this life. He is determined that we have a chance for this freedom. Although we will never experience absolute freedom this side of heaven, if we are willing to cooperate with His plan, we can experience much more than we could ever imagine.

This will be a process. It will only occur as we are willing to go to a deeper level in our relationship with Him. There will be struggles and many failures along the way. However, the Father does not get tired of being there to bring us to victory. The only question is, Are we willing to go with Him?

Have you ever known God to answer a prayer before you even asked, or to provide for you before you even knew what you needed? What does it mean to you that God is working in your life even when you are unaware of it?

What does it mean for you to go to a deeper level in your relationship with God?

Think about the past twenty-four hours. On reflection, what evidence do you see of God working in your life?

We don't usually walk around thinking about our own self-worth. We usually walk around thinking about how to respond to the moment and people before us. Have you noticed a connection between your worth and your moments? How do they relate right now?

Take a moment to think about how much you've grown in terms of cooperating with God as He helps you mature spiritually. How has your connection with God changed over the course of the last month? Are you more aware of your partnership with Him in this thing called your life?

TALK TO GOD

God, when I try to get life "right" on my own, I end up feeling so alone. Help me relax in Your love. Help me accept my human limitations and be grateful for Your forgiveness. I feel like a child who has to wear himself out struggling before he'll relax in his dad's arms. Teach me to relax in Your forgiveness and acceptance. Amen.

SO, YOU THINK YOU'RE CLOSE TO PERFECT?

Whoever believes that Jesus is the Christ is born of God, and everyone who loves Him who begot also loves him who is begotten of Him. By this we know that we love the children of God, when we love God and keep His commandments. For this is the love of God, that we keep His commandments. And His commandments are not burdensome. For whatever is born of God overcomes the world. And this is the victory that has overcome the world—our faith. Who is he who overcomes the world, but he who believes that Jesus is the Son of God?

—1 John 5:1–5

OVERCOMING HOPELESSNESS

> **What does it mean to you to "overcome the world"? What kind of personal victory does that entail?**

The fear of failure can affect our lives in many ways. One of the most common symptoms of the fear of failure is perfectionism, an unwillingness to fail. Another very common result of the fear of failure is a willingness to be involved in only those activities that can be done well. New challenges are avoided at all costs. Anger is another normal response. What is the common first thing to do when we realize we have failed? We look for someone to blame. Experiencing failure and fearing failure can lead to deep depression. Much of what is known as low motivation or laziness is better understood as hopelessness that comes when people believe they will fail.

How would you define perfectionism? What evidence of it (or of your response to it) do you see in your life?

Are you a person who fears new challenges? What connection do you trace between that fear (or lack of it) and your deepest sense of worth?

Think of a time in the past twenty-four hours when you felt hopeless. If you need to think back further, go ahead and focus for a minute on that hopeless time. What was your view of yourself during that time?

What was God's view of you during that time?

Why do you think the myth "If we just try hard enough, we'll be good enough" is so hard to let go?

TALK TO GOD

Father, who taught me the myth that if I try hard enough I'll be good enough? Somehow I've come to believe that I can get to a place where I don't need You. I might not say it, but I live that way sometimes. Keep me from the land called Denial. Help me to see myself realistically and to see the truth of who You are. Amen.

WHY DOES A PUPPY LEARN TO OBEY?

What then? Shall we sin because we are not under law but under grace? Certainly not! Do you not know that to whom you present yourselves slaves to obey, you are that one's slaves whom you obey, whether of sin leading to death, or of obedience leading to righteousness? But God be thanked that though you were slaves of sin, yet you obeyed from the heart that form of doctrine to which you were delivered. And having been set free from sin, you became slaves of righteousness.

—ROMANS 6:15–18

OBEYING TO PLEASE GOD

> **Think about the people whom you would most like to please. What would you like them to say about you?**

Satan has effectively blinded man to the painful, damaging consequences of sin. Sooner or later, sin will result in some form of destruction. Our loving Father has given us the Holy Spirit to convict us of sin. On the cross, Jesus bore all the punishment we deserved; therefore, we no longer need to fear punishment from God for our sins. We have a wrong perspective if we only view God's commands as restrictions. We must realize that His commands are guidelines, given so that we might enjoy life to the fullest. Obedience to God's commands should never be considered a means to gain His approval. Our noblest motivation for serving Christ is simply that He is worthy of our love and obedience.

In what ways are you motivated by the sheer fact of pleasing God who already loves you more than you can understand?

How would you explain to someone else why you obey God?

How do you define sin? Sin is not always necessarily just wrong deeds. Sometimes it's being less than God calls us to be, "missing the mark." How do you define the damage that is done in your life by sin in this broader sense of the word?

Think of a time when you felt really good about yourself. Jot down the circumstances. Then think of a low time in your life. Jot down those circumstances. How was your view of sin affected during those times?

TALK TO GOD

Father, I think I dishonor You when I cower away as if You wait to condemn me. Forgive me for treating You like a school principal in that way. Teach me to enjoy the freedom of Your love while honoring our relationship enough to take seriously the commands You give for my own benefit. I worship You. Amen.

HOW MANY PEOPLE CAN YOU KEEP HAPPY AT ONE TIME?

The LORD is on my side; I will not fear. What can man do to me? The LORD is for me among those who help me; therefore I shall see my desire on those who hate me. It is better to trust in the LORD than to put confidence in man. It is better to trust in the LORD than to put confidence in princes.

—PSALM 118:6–9

The fear of man brings a snare, but whoever trusts in the LORD shall be safe.

—PROVERBS 29:25

AVOIDING THE "PLEASING" PITFALL

> **Think about a time (recently if possible) when someone responded to you negatively. What kinds of feelings did that stir up in you about yourself? About them?**

Living according to the false belief *I must be approved by certain others to feel good about myself* causes us to fear rejection, conforming virtually all of our attitudes and actions to the expectations of others. We can ultimately seek either the approval of men or the approval of God as the basis of our self-worth. We cannot seek both.

God wants to be the Lord of our lives, and He is unwilling to share that rightful lordship with anyone else. Therefore, the only way we can overcome the fear of rejection is to value the constant approval of God over the conditional approval of people. The good news is that because we are fully pleasing to God, we need not be devastated when others respond to us in a negative way.

Virtually all of us fear rejection. Rejection won't usually physically hurt us, so what is it we really fear? What do you fear most about rejection?

How does knowing that you are completely and totally pleasing to God help you overcome the fear of rejection?

Psalm 118:6–9 says it's better to put your confidence in God than in people. You've spent a lot of time the last few weeks giving thought to this concept. What still makes it tough to step back from people's opinions and put your confidence in God alone?

What does it feel like to let go of the responsibility of keeping someone else happy?

From your experiences, what happens when you let the people around you take responsibility for their own happiness and you take care of yours?

TALK TO GOD

Father, it does feel so good when I keep the people around me happy. It's nice to be without the hassle of conflict. Unfortunately, I have lost some of myself to make that happen. I see Your vision of me walking authentically through life content in the fact that I am pleasing to You rather than pleasing the people I pass by. I just need Your help to keep living that out one step at a time. Amen.

CAN YOU HAVE TOO MANY BROTHERS AND SISTERS?

For as the body is one and has many members, but all the members of that one body, being many, are one body, so also is Christ. For by one Spirit we were all baptized into one body—whether Jews or Greeks, whether slaves or free—and have all been made to drink into one Spirit. For in fact the body is not one member but many.

If the foot should say, "Because I am not a hand, I am not of the body," is it therefore not of the body? And if the ear should say, "Because I am not an eye, I am not of the body," is it therefore not of the body? If the whole body were an eye, where would be the hearing? If the whole were hearing, where would be the smelling? But now God has set the members, each one of them, in the body just as He pleased.

—1 CORINTHIANS 12:12–18

LIVING IN THE BODY

> **Who are the people you turn to for spiritual encouragement? How are they most effective in encouraging you spiritually?**

While God often demonstrates His love and affirmation for us through believers and nonbelievers alike, His desire is that our relationships with others will enable us to know Him more fully. His work through others is, in part, to serve as a channel through which we can better understand His divine love and acceptance of us. Sadly, we are all prone to miss His message and mistake His messenger(s) as the source of our fulfillment.

Our relationships with one another are very important to God, so much so that He has placed unity among the brethren as a priority in our relationship with Him (Matt. 5:23–24). This is because God has reconciled us to Himself as a body in Christ (Eph. 2:16) and therefore intends for us to interact as members of one another (Eph 4:25).

What do you see as God's purpose for the church?

How does the metaphor in 1 Corinthians 12:12–18 (the church of Christ functioning together as body parts do) work with your understanding of the church?

We've already established that we can't base our significance on the opinions of others, even other Christians. So what role do your brothers and sisters in Christ have in terms of your value?

Think about the last time you were at church. What did you have to offer there? How did it make you feel?

What would you like your role to be in the body of Christ?

TALK TO GOD

Father, I know You have a great plan for the church. Thank You for that plan. But sometimes the church is the very place where hurts and wounds occur. Help me to see past that and keep my eye on Your purposes for Your body. Help me not to try to live out my life of faith in isolation. Give me Your vision for Your body in this world. Amen.

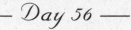

— Day 56 —

WHO NAMED YOU
JUDGE AND JURY?

And you have forgotten the exhortation which speaks to you as to sons:

*"My son, do not despise the chastening of the LORD, nor be
discouraged when you are rebuked by Him; for whom the LORD
loves He chastens, and scourges every son whom He receives."*

*If you endure chastening, God deals with you as with sons; for what
son is there whom a father does not chasten? But if you are without
chastening, of which all have become partakers, then you are illegitimate
and not sons. Furthermore, we have had human fathers who corrected
us, and we paid them respect. Shall we not much more readily be in
subjection to the Father of spirits and live? For they indeed for a few
days chastened us as seemed best to them, but He for our profit, that
we may be partakers of His holiness. Now no chastening seems to be
joyful for the present, but painful; nevertheless, afterward it yields the
peaceable fruit of righteousness to those who have been trained by it.*

— HEBREWS 12:5–11

PUNISHING VERSUS DISCIPLINING

We punish a child when we apply negative consequences for
bad behavior. We *discipline* a child when we help him learn
how to replace bad behavior with good behavior, walking him
through the process. Sometimes they feel the same to the child,
but for us it is a different intention and process. Do you most
often perceive God's *punishment* (which was actually taken on
by Christ) or His *discipline?*

Many of us operate on the theory that if we are hard enough on ourselves, then God won't have to punish us. We fail to realize that God disciplines us in love and never punishes us in anger. Because God loves us unconditionally and does not punish us, we don't need to punish ourselves.

The blame game leaves us feeling all alone without experiencing the faith we need to live without fear. Fear and faith can never be coequal. One will always dominate the other. The more you give yourself to fear, the more difficult it is to experience faith in your life.

The fear of punishment and the desire to punish others can be overcome by realizing that Christ has borne the punishment we deserve. His motives toward us are loving and kind. His discipline is designed to correct us and protect us from the destruction of sin, not to punish us.

If God disciplines us to teach a new way of life, what is our best response to His discipline?

How do you tell the difference between the natural consequences of your choices, even mistakes, and the discipline of God?

If God's discipline is really training in life, what message does that send to our sense of significance?

Think about yesterday. Did you feel God teaching you, training you, or guiding you? What did it feel like?

TALK TO GOD

When I get a moment of clarity, Father, I realize how futile it is for me to be hard on myself to settle a score that You've already settled. I don't know what game I'm playing that makes me want to punish myself on Your behalf. But I guess that is the tricky nature of false beliefs. Thank You for continuing to show me the truth. Help me live according to it. What a better life, when I stay there! Amen.

HAVE I KICKED MYSELF ENOUGH TODAY?

Blessed be the God and Father of our Lord Jesus Christ, who has blessed us with every spiritual blessing in the heavenly places in Christ, just as He chose us in Him before the foundation of the world, that we should be holy and without blame before Him in love, having predestined us to adoption as sons by Jesus Christ to Himself, according to the good pleasure of His will, to the praise of the glory of His grace, by which He made us accepted in the Beloved.

In Him we have redemption through His blood, the forgiveness of sins, according to the riches of His grace.

—EPHESIANS 1:3–7

PAYING PENANCE

Penance is punishment, often self-inflicted. It's not the same as repentance. Repentance is turning away from sin. Penance is punishing yourself for sin. God wants our repentance, requires it even. He doesn't have much use for our penance. How much energy do you give to each?

There have been times when I thought that I couldn't feel forgiven until I had experienced remorse for my sin for a certain period of time. These occasions led to depression because I could hardly complete my penance for one sin before I had sinned again. Then I would have to feel bad about that for a period of time, only to sin again . . . and again . . . and again . . . and . . . well, you get the picture.

No matter how much we do to make up for our sin, we will continue to feel guilty and believe that we need to do more unless we resist Satan, the accuser of the brethren. This can only be accomplished because Christ's blood has completely paid for our sins and delivered us from guilt. We need to verbalize what the blood of Christ has done for us: We are deeply loved, completely forgiven, fully pleasing, totally accepted, and complete in Christ.

How would you expect a person to behave who was "deeply loved, completely forgiven, fully pleasing, totally accepted, and complete in Christ"?

No matter how your life is going right now, the truth is that you already are all of those things listed above. Taking each description one by one, list how closely you perceive yourself to fit the description.

Ephesians 1:3–7 says that God chose you before the foundation of the world was established. You are significant in the grand scheme of things. What feelings or thoughts does that truth raise in you?

Why is it more attractive to us to earn our own way instead of receiving grace from God?

TALK TO GOD

I guess, God, that sometimes I'm like a little kid at the cash register. You've paid for the whole basketful, but I keep taking the change out of my pocket as if I have enough to pay myself. In this moment, I lay down my own foolishness. Thank You for Your provision for my very soul. Thank You for doing what I could never do for myself. Amen.

— *Day 58* —

IS WHAT YOU SEE REALLY WHAT YOU GET?

For this reason I bow my knees to the Father of our Lord Jesus Christ, from whom the whole family in heaven and earth is named, that He would grant you, according to the riches of His glory, to be strengthened with might through His Spirit in the inner man, that Christ may dwell in your hearts through faith; that you, being rooted and grounded in love, may be able to comprehend with all the saints what is the width and length and depth and height—to know the love of Christ which passes knowledge; that you may be filled with all the fullness of God.

Now to Him who is able to do exceedingly abundantly above all that we ask or think, according to the power that works in us, to Him be glory in the church by Christ Jesus to all generations, forever and ever. Amen.

—EPHESIANS 3:14–21

FINDING TRUE BEAUTY

How well do you think you measure up in your culture as far as looks? Be honest. How does that affect the value you place on yourself?

Beauty is highly valued in our society. Television commercials and programs, magazine ads, and billboards all convey the message that beauty is to be prized. But very few of us compare to the beautiful people we see in these ads and programs, and most of us are ashamed of at least one aspect of our appearance. We spend hundreds of dollars and an inestimable amount of time and worry covering up or altering our skin, eyes, teeth, faces, noses, thighs, and scalps, refusing to believe that God, in His sovereignty and love, gave us the features He wants us to have.

Sometimes oil will wash up on a beautiful ocean beach to form a tarlike substance. When this happens the tar can easily transfer onto our feet, staining our feet to the extent that sometimes we wonder if we will ever get rid of the stain. Shame is the emotional tar of our lives. Unlike the beach tar, we can't get rid of it without an act of God.

Tar-stained feet . . . Do you have blotches of shame or inferiority that you are having a hard time getting rid of? Describe them.

What is your prayer in regard to the areas of your life that are still a source of shame to you?

In Ephesians 3:14–21 Paul prays that the Christians at Ephesus will be "filled with all the fullness of God." In what areas of your life are you filled with the fullness of God? In what areas do you still feel you're running on fumes?

Think back over your physical appearance in the past twenty-four hours. How big a part did it play in your sense of significance?

There will always be things we don't like about our lives. There will always be things we would change if we could. The essential thing is that we don't connect our worth to those things. What difficulties about your life or yourself keep getting connected to your sense of significance?

TALK TO GOD

Father, You formed my shape. You put me in a world where the outside is the cover by which every book is judged. Give me Your wisdom to judge my worth by a completely different standard than just how my body compares to this world of airbrushed photos. Give me eyes to see the needs of my soul and the beauty that You want to cultivate there. Amen.

WOULD YOU RATHER HAVE FAITH OR A MOUTHFUL OF WATER?

And Peter answered Him and said, "Lord, if it is You, command me to come to You on the water."

So He said, "Come." And when Peter had come down out of the boat, he walked on the water to go to Jesus. But when he saw that the wind was boisterous, he was afraid; and beginning to sink he cried out, saying, "Lord, save me!"

And immediately Jesus stretched out His hand and caught him, and said to him, "O you of little faith, why did you doubt?" And when they got into the boat, the wind ceased.

Then those who were in the boat came and worshiped Him, saying, "Truly You are the Son of God."

—Matthew 14:28–33

CONFESSING YOUR WEAKNESSES

How would you compare your faith journey to Peter's? Have there been times when you felt as if you were walking on water? Falling into the waves? Feeling God's hand pull you back up?

When we do sin, we should follow King David's example. When Nathan confronted David about his sin of adultery with Bathsheba,

David did not run from his sin or its consequences. Confess your sins, worship God, and get on with your life. You can experience the mercy of God no matter what you've been through.

Our greatest obstacle to experiencing regeneration is that we don't look different and sometimes we don't act much differently. As we recognize the results of justification, reconciliation, and propitiation, we will find it much easier to hold to the fact that we have undergone regeneration. However, it will come down to whether or not we're willing to accept what God reveals about our true natures. He is not lying to us, and He is not deceived.

How important is it to you to be right? How difficult is it for anyone, even God, to point out that you need to change?

When was the last time you had to admit you were wrong to someone? How did it go?

Why does accepting help, admitting weakness, or admitting you were wrong often threaten your sense of significance? What does that reveal about your beliefs?

Think of a time when you felt God "speaking" to you or leading you. How did you recognize His voice?

TALK TO GOD

Father, it makes so much sense to walk through life believing Your voice more than any other. I guess my human nature will always struggle a bit with putting my focus on the voices around me, but I pray that You'll always call me back to You. Help me to listen. I believe that Your love is the steady force in my life. Help me make Your voice the steady one I hear in my head and heart. Thanks for Your mercy. Amen.

WHERE IS IT YOU THINK YOU'RE GOING?

But we are bound to give thanks to God always for you, brethren beloved by the Lord, because God from the beginning chose you for salvation through sanctification by the Spirit and belief in the truth, to which He called you by our gospel, for the obtaining of the glory of our Lord Jesus Christ. Therefore, brethren, stand fast and hold the traditions which you were taught, whether by word or our epistle.

Now may our Lord Jesus Christ Himself, and our God and Father, who has loved us and given us everlasting consolation and good hope by grace, comfort your hearts and establish you in every good word and work.

—2 Thessalonians 2:13–17

REDEFINING THE JOURNEY

In what ways do you feel as though you are "established in every good word and work"?

Allow me to summarize the four great doctrines we have been pointing to as the solution for the four false beliefs:

Because of justification, you are completely forgiven and fully pleasing to God. You no longer have to fear failure.

Because of reconciliation, you are totally accepted by God. You no longer have to fear rejection.

Because of propitiation, you are deeply loved by God. You no longer have to fear punishment; nor do you have to punish others.

Because of regeneration, you have been made brand-new, complete in Christ. You no longer need to experience the pain of shame.

The more we understand and apply the truths of justification, propitiation, reconciliation, and regeneration, the more our lives will reflect His character. Spiritual growth is not magic. It comes as we apply the love and forgiveness of Christ in our daily circumstances. It comes as we reflect on the unconditional acceptance of Christ and His awesome power and choose to respond to situations and people in light of His sovereign purpose and kindness toward us.

"Spiritual growth is not magic." How do you respond to that statement?

What have you learned during the last couple of months about applying the love and forgiveness of Christ in your daily circumstances?

How would you describe God's kindness toward you?

What change have you made in your life in regard to where you find your source of significance? What difference has that made in your life?

Write your own prayer thanking God for your relationship with Him and asking Him for help as you continue to trust that relationship for your sense of significance.

TALK TO GOD

Holy God, I am Yours. I matter to You. It is within our relationship that I find my most basic meaning in life. Teach me to base my life on our relationship. Help me to continue to see clearly my false beliefs about what makes me worth something. Help me build a life based on Your truth. Amen and Amen.

Continue the Search...

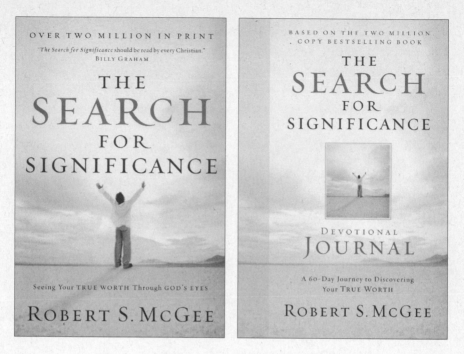

Also available in audio cassette and CD

Coming in December 2003
The Search for Significance Student Edition